easy to make!

Wheat Free

Good Housekeeping

easy to make!
Wheat Free

COLLINS & BROWN

First published in Great Britain in 2008
by Collins & Brown
10 Southcombe Street
London W14 0RA

An imprint of Anova Books Company Ltd.

The Good Housekeeping website is
www.goodhousekeeping.co.uk

10 9 8 7 6 5 4 3 2

ISBN 978-1-84340-467-5

A catalogue record for this book is available from the British
Library.

Reproduction by Dot Gradations Ltd
Printed and bound by SNP Leefung, China

Keep updated. Email food@anovabooks.com

This book can be ordered direct from the publisher. Contact the
marketing department, but try your bookshop first.

www.anovabooks.com

NOTES

- Both metric and imperial measures are given for the recipes. Follow either set of measures, not a mixture of both, as they are not interchangeable.
- All spoon measures are level.
  1 tsp = 5ml spoon; 1 tbsp = 15ml spoon.
- Ovens and grills must be preheated to the specified temperature.
- Use sea salt and freshly ground black pepper unless otherwise suggested.
- Fresh herbs should be used unless dried herbs are specified in a recipe.
- Medium eggs should be used except where otherwise specified. Free-range eggs are recommended.
- Note that certain recipes, including mayonnaise, lemon curd and some cold desserts, contain raw or lightly cooked eggs. The young, elderly, pregnant women and anyone with an immune-deficiency disease should avoid these, because of the slight risk of salmonella.
- Calorie, fat and carbohydrate counts per serving are provided for the recipes.

Picture Credits
Photographers: Nicky Dowey (pages 33, 34, 38, 39, 40, 41, 44, 45, 48, 50, 53, 54, 57, 58, 64, 65, 68, 69, 70, 72, 74, 77, 80, 81, 82, 85, 87, 93, 94, 96, 102, 103, 107, 109, 114, 116, 117, 119, 122, 123 and 126); Will Heap (pages 49, 55, 61, 63, 73, 78, 84, 88, 92, 108, 112, 113 and 120); David Munns (page 124); Craig Robertson (all Basics photography); Roger Stowell (page 98); Clive Streeter (page 99); Lucinda Symons (pages 32, 35, 37, 46, 51, 56, 60, 75, 79, 89, 97, 101 and 104)
Stylist: Helen Trent
Home Economists: Emma Jane Frost and Teresa Goldfinch

Contents

Foreword

Whether it's to lose weight or for health reasons, a wheat-free diet is now a way of life for many people. While a number of everyday foods are off-limits, there's no need to feel deprived: you can even have that slice of toast in the morning! *Wheat Free* is packed with quick and easy recipes that don't contain wheat products. Making inventive use of alternative grains such as rice, polenta, barley and quinoa, recipes include a simple yet luxurious asparagus risotto and a wonderful sticky lemon polenta cake. Many of the recipes are suitable for coeliacs – who have to avoid all gluten – as well as for anyone with a wheat intolerance, whether it's mild or severe. The clearly written introduction explains how to adapt to a wheat-free lifestyle and outlines all the foods you can enjoy when you can't eat wheat, and the recipes ease you through the day, with ideas for breakfasts, soups, salads and suppers – as well as some super desserts, cakes and biscuits – to make cutting out wheat as effortless as possible.

We've gathered together 101 ways to make light work of eating wheat-free. All the recipes have been triple tested in the Good Housekeeping kitchens to make sure they work every time.

Emma

Emma Marsden
Cookery Editor
Good Housekeeping

0

The Basics

What is food intolerance?

Food intolerance is an inability to tolerate a particular food or foods. Put simply, it means the food doesn't suit you, and causes detrimental physical side effects and general malabsorption of foods. It may be mild or severe, and can happen at any stage in your life. Wheat and lactose intolerance are two of the most common food intolerances; other foods regularly cited include shellfish, citrus fruits, and tree nuts such as Brazil nuts.

What causes it?

No one knows for sure what causes food intolerances. As far as wheat is concerned, many health specialists believe that the overdependence on wheat in our diet – eating too much bread, pasta and pizzas, for example – and the fact that most of the wheat we eat is highly processed, are major contributing factors. In short, our diets are overloaded with wheat. The good news is that by excluding the offending food, the food intolerance can in time be reversed or significantly improved so that you can tolerate small amounts of it without any debilitating effects. An intolerance may also be transient and children, for example, may 'grow out of' their wheat intolerance.

Food intolerance or food allergy?

Unlike food intolerance, where symptoms may take a few days to show themselves and may not be clear-cut, an allergic reaction is a specific immunological reaction and is usually immediate. Common allergic reactions include itchy skin, and swelling of the mouth and throat. In extreme cases, this swelling may result in anaphylaxis. A food allergy cannot be reversed, and will need to be properly diagnosed by your GP or a medically qualified allergy specialist. The only way to combat its effects is to completely exclude the offending food from your diet for life. It is estimated that in the UK up to 15% of the population report adverse food reactions, and that 1–4% of the general population and 6% of children suffer from food allergies.

Wheat intolerance or gluten intolerance?

Gluten intolerance is an inability to tolerate gluten, a protein found in wheat, rye and barley (it is also found to a lesser degree in oats, though research shows that oats from uncontaminated sources may often be tolerated). It is a chronic, lifelong, genetically linked medical condition, and it causes coeliac disease – inflammation of the intestinal lining or, more rarely, the skin rash dermatitis herpetiformis (DH). It affects all ages, including infants, and sufferers must practise strict avoidance of these grains and eat a gluten-free diet for life. The Coeliac Society estimates that 1% of the population are coeliacs.

Unlike wheat intolerance, gluten intolerance is not reversible.

Take professional advice

In reality, because the symptoms are so similar and the main sources of gluten are wheat and wheat products, it is often difficult to distinguish between gluten intolerance and wheat intolerance. There are many people who feel they are wheat intolerant who may actually be gluten intolerant. That is why, if you feel you may be suffering from a food intolerance, it is important to undergo a proper diagnosis with a properly qualified allergy specialist/gastroenterologist arranged by your GP.

Common symptoms of wheat intolerance

Many of the following symptoms are not exclusive to wheat intolerance, but if you regularly suffer from some of them with no obvious reason why, then wheat may be a cause. Unlike gluten intolerance, the symptoms may come and go.

- Bloating*
- Fatigue, lack of energy, and general tiredness*
- Foggy thinking*
- Flatulence
- IBS (Irritable Bowel Syndrome)
- Headaches
- Constipation/diarrhoea
- Feeling below par
- Lack of motivation, general negativity, depression
- Fluctuating weight
- Craving for wheat

*Symptoms most commonly associated with wheat intolerance

How do I know if I am wheat intolerant?

The simplest way to assess whether you may be intolerant of wheat is to use the recipes in this book to help you exclude all wheat and wheat products from your diet, and to monitor any lessening of symptoms. You must be rigorous and will need to follow a wheat-free diet for around four weeks to give your body the chance to 'detoxify' properly. Seek medical advice if necessary first.

- Keep a food diary for at least one week before you adopt your wheat-free diet, writing down what you eat, and any symptoms.
- While on your wheat-free diet, continue your diary and monitor symptoms.
- You may initially experience headaches, or feel worse when you start your wheat-free regime. Don't worry: this is a common reaction to detoxification and it is temporary.
- At the end of four weeks, gradually reintroduce wheat into your diet: choose 100% wheat products – pasta, bread, and so on, and monitor your body's reaction, eating a little more of the food every day for at least three days. If you get a reaction, stop eating wheat.

If your symptoms improve, and you have an adverse reaction when reintroducing wheat, seek medical advice to confirm your diagnosis and whether you are intolerant to wheat or gluten.

What next?

Learning more about food intolerances and how changing your diet can affect your health for the better will help you enormously in planning your own wheat-free lifestyle. For where to start, see below.

Adapting to a wheat-free diet

Eating a wheat-free diet could not be simpler. Major supermarkets, health food stores and organic shops stock a wide range of wheat-free products, including breakfast cereals, flours, breads, pasta, cakes and biscuits. Supermarkets also produce lists of their own-label wheat-free products. Expert advice and help, as well as sources of wheat- and gluten-free products, are easy to find on the internet, wheat-free cookery courses are common, and because many people today are wheat intolerant, or prefer not to include wheat in their diet, you – and your children – should have little difficulty in eating out, and no need to feel awkward at parties and other social occasions. Adapting meals and recipes is also very easy – for more advice, see page 16.

Getting started

A wheat-free diet has much to commend it, and can be a great opportunity to change your life for the better. Even for those who can eat wheat, building wheat-free meals into your diet adds variety and gives your digestion a welcome break. Below are the foods to avoid and those you can enjoy.

Which foods should I avoid?

It is important to learn which common foods contain wheat, and therefore should be eliminated from your diet. They are:

- ✗ All wheat flours and products derived from wheat: sprouted wheat grains, wheatgerm, wheat bran, semolina, bulgur, couscous
- ✗ All breads, pizzas, pastas and noodles containing wheat flour
- ✗ All muesli that contains wheat flakes or bran flakes; breakfast cereals containing wheat or wheat bran – for example, Shredded Wheat, Weetabix, Bran Flakes
- ✗ All pastry, including filo pastry, cakes, biscuits, crackers and pretzels, except those which specifically state on the label that they are wheat-free
- ✗ Pancakes, tortillas, pittas, chappatis, naan bread, poppadoms
- ✗ All sausages, except 100% meat sausages, and those that specifically state on the label that they are wheat- or gluten-free
- ✗ All foods coated in breadcrumbs (such as fish fingers and fishcakes); stuffings containing breadcrumbs, and gratins with bread toppings
- ✗ All foods coated in batter, such as traditional fried fish and Japanese tempura
- ✗ Sauces, soups, desserts, condiments, confectionery and snacks containing flour or wheat starch
- ✗ Soy (shoyu) sauce and miso made from wheat
- ✗ Beers and lagers, where wheat is used in the brewing process

Which foods can I eat?

A wheat-free diet is a wonderful opportunity to discover many delicious foods that you may not have included in your diet previously and so, far from feeling deprived, many people find that a wheat-free diet is a very rewarding and exciting way to eat. The list of foods you can enjoy is as varied as you want to make it. These are the foods you can safely eat on a wheat-free diet:

- ✓ Dairy products
- ✓ Fish
- ✓ Meat
- ✓ Vegetables, salads and fruit
- ✓ Tofu products
- ✓ Dried beans and pulses
- ✓ Nuts and seeds
- ✓ Dried fruits
- ✓ Herbs and spices
- ✓ Quorn
- ✓ Grains: rice (all varieties), barley, millet, amaranth, quinoa, buckwheat, sago, sorghum, tapioca
- ✓ All products made from maize (corn): tortilla chips, tacos, polenta, corn breads, corn crispbreads, popcorn
- ✓ All products made from oats: porridge, flapjacks, oat biscuits, oatmeal, oatbran
- ✓ Rice cakes, rice noodles
- ✓ Buckwheat pancakes and Japanese 100% soba noodles (made from buckwheat flour)
- ✓ All products made from chickpea (gram) flour, e.g. falafel, onion bhajis
- ✓ Asian glass or cellophane noodles (made from pea and bean flour)
- ✓ Flour: oat, barley, maize, gram, soya, sago, tapioca, rice, arrowroot, potato, cornflour
- ✓ All prepared foods that specifically state on the label that they are wheat-free

Which breads can I eat?

- ✓ 100% rye breads, crispbreads and crackers
- ✓ German pumpernickel and wheat-free grain breads
- ✓ Home-made wheat-free breads
- ✓ All manufactured breads that specifically state on the label that they are wheat-free
- ✓ Gluten-free breads are usually wheat-free also

Note: Many gluten-free breads are expensive and white breads in particular can contain a wide range of processing aids and ingredients. Choose natural rye bread, wheat-free wholegrain breads, or home-made gluten-free breads as your everyday bread. When buying breads, choose organic breads when you can.

What about spelt and kamut?

These are little-known but very nutritious varieties of wheat. People who are sensitive to common bread wheat, *Triticum vulgare*, or who have wheat intolerance (as opposed to the more serious wheat allergy), often find that they can eat spelt and kamut. Spelt and kamut breads, pastas and breakfast cereals are all available.

Note: Because spelt and kamut contain gluten, they are not suitable for gluten-free diets, and must be avoided by coeliacs and people with gluten intolerance.

What about processed food and ready-prepared meals?

This is a much more difficult area, primarily because common processing aids, particularly thickeners and fillers, are often wheat based and can be found hidden in the most unlikely foods and ingredients – for example, yogurts, mustard powder and spice mixtures, mayonnaise, stock cubes, sauces and condiments, including tomato sauce, as well as meat products such as sausages, burgers, meat patties, and cooked meats. As a general rule, keep processed foods and ready-prepared foods to a minimum. For preference, also choose brands that specialise in wheat-free products. If your intolerance is severe, only buy those products that state on the label that they are wheat-free.

Tips

Read all labels very carefully: look for 'wheat-free'.
Avoid foods that include rusk, modified starch (or corn), wheat starch, hydrolized wheat protein, wheat gluten, or raising agents containing wheat starch on the ingredients list.
Organic wheat-free products will have fewer processing aids.
If in any doubt, choose another product or make your own!

What about gluten-free products?

Generally, foods that are gluten-free are safe for wheat-free diets. However, gluten-free products may also contain wheat starch or other wheat proteins, which, depending on the severity of the wheat intolerance, may cause aggravation. Check labels very carefully, and to be absolutely sure, choose products that state that they are wheat-free as well as gluten-free.

Successful wheat-free eating

Build your diet around fresh foods that are wheat-free. **Eat regular meals.**
Plan ahead: take fruit, a ripe avocado, wheat-free nut and seed bars, and healthy wheat-free snacks such as falafels with you to snack on when you go out.
For a packed lunch, try salad, hummus or other dips and crudités, or wholegrain wheat-free sandwiches, or take a flask of soup.
When eating out, check that the dishes you have chosen do not contain hidden wheat.
Don't think deprivation, think liberation!

Ten steps to health

Changing to a wheat-free diet will help you feel better and healthier. Incorporating your new, wheat-free way of eating into a healthy lifestyle, by following the simple steps below, will set you up for life and ensure you achieve maximum health and vitality.

1. Water

Water is the elixir of life and is nature's prime detoxifier. Aim to drink at least 1 litre (1³/₄ pints) per day, or preferably 1–2 litres (1³/₄–3¹/₂ pints).

2. Vegetables, salads and fruit

Make sure your diet contains plenty of these. Not only are they a storehouse of vitamins and minerals, but they also help balance acidic foods such as dairy products and proteins, thus keeping the body at its optimum pH, which is slightly alkaline.

3. Superfood good carbs

Make sure your diet contains plenty of complex, unrefined, good carbohydrates such as whole grains, pulses, nuts and seeds. These foods will sustain your energy levels and help maintain your ideal weight.

4. Superfood good fats

Fats are essential to all life processes and a low-fat diet is not a good idea for long-term health. The trick is to replace bad fats (saturated fats, hydrogenated vegetable fats and oils) with omega-rich unsaturated fats, which are found in certain vegetable oils. Nuts, seeds and oily fish are also good sources of omega fats.

5. Eat regularly

Skipping meals leads to energy dips, stresses your system and is a sure-fire way to put on weight. Eating regularly keeps your physical and mental energy levels steady, preventing hunger pangs and the desire to snack.

6. Avoid processed foods

Most processed foods contain hidden wheat or gluten in the form of modified starch, so it is vital for anyone allergic to wheat or gluten to avoid them. Generally, too, the more your diet contains fresh, unprocessed 'real' foods, the better it is for your health.

7. Variety

Enjoy as wide a variety of foods as possible. This way you will ensure that your diet contains all the health-giving micronutrients it needs for optimum health. It also lessens the likelihood of your developing food intolerances to particular foods.

8. Exercise regularly

Exercise is vital. It energises you, raises your metabolic rate, helps you to maintain your correct weight, reduces stress and helps you sleep better.

9. Stress less

Stress comes in all shapes and sizes, whether it is pressure at work, noise, traffic or the constant barrage of environmental and electronic pollution. Reduce stress by learning some simple deep-breathing techniques.

10. Sleep

Sleep is Nature's happy pill, the ultimate physical and mental reviver, and the secret to staying young. Make getting enough sleep a top priority.

In the kitchen

Cooking wheat-free food generally requires minimal changes in the kitchen. If you're worried about what to use instead of wheat, look no further than the table on the right to find out what to substitute in its place. You don't need to miss out on favourites like pasta and pizza, just plan ahead and learn a few simple rules.

Regular food	Wheat-free substitute
Breadcrumbs:	**Maize** (polenta) gives a delicious crispy coating to foods such as fishcakes and fried chicken.
Couscous and bulgur:	**Quinoa** (see page 24). It is nutritious, easy to cook and delicious. Use it for all couscous and bulgur recipes. A great choice, too, for pilafs and salads.
Crumbles:	**Oatmeal or oatflakes**, or a mixture of oatmeal and ground nuts, makes a nutritious crumble topping.
Flour:	**Use rice flour** for lining cake and bread tins; use gluten-free flour for dusting meat and fish.
Pasta:	**Wheat-free pastas** can be used for all recipes (see page 17).
Pizza base:	**Ready-made gluten-free base**, or make your own using gluten-free flour.
Sandwiches:	**Rye breads** and German-style wheat-free grain breads make sandwiches packed with good carbs.
Snacks:	**Rice cakes** and corn and rye crispbreads are perfect.
Wraps and pancakes:	**Try rice pancakes**, substituting ground brown or white rice flour for wheat flour in your usual recipe, or buckwheat pancakes, using wheat-free buckwheat pancake mix.

Round tin

1. Put the tin on a sheet of greaseproof paper and draw a circle around its circumference. Cut out the circle just inside the drawn line.

2. Cut a strip or strips about 2cm (³/₄in) wider than the depth of the tin and fold up one long edge of each strip by 1cm (¹/₂in). Make cuts, about 2.5cm (1in) apart, through the folded edge of the strip(s) up to the fold line.

3. Lightly grease the tin with butter, making sure it is completely coated.

4. Press the strip(s) on to the sides of the tin so that the snipped edge sits on the base.

5. Lay the circle in the bottom of the tin and grease the paper.

Storecupboard

If you are allergic to wheat you must ensure that all spices, spice pastes, sweet and savoury bottled sauces, condiments, soy sauce and miso, canned goods, beers and lager are wheat-free. Read the labels carefully to check. It is a good idea to choose brands that do not contain wheat fillers or thickeners.

Wheat-free pastas All gluten-free pastas are suitable for wheat-free diets, and there is a wide range to choose from, all varying slightly in taste, depending on the flour they are made from. The main difference between wheat-free and wheat pasta is that wheat-free pasta becomes too soft very quickly, so you need to watch cooking times very closely, and drain the pasta immediately after cooking.

Thickeners Arrowroot, cornflour, potato flour and wheat-free thickening granules made from potato flour, available in supermarkets, can be used instead of flour to thicken savoury and sweet dishes. Unlike wheat flour, they are usually mixed in a little water (slaked) before being added to the dish. Follow the instructions on the packet.

Loaf tin

1. Lightly grease the tin with butter, making sure it is completely coated.

2. Cut out a sheet of greaseproof paper to the same length as the base and wide enough to cover both the base and the long sides. Press it into position, making sure that it sits snugly in the corners.

3. Now cut another sheet to the same width as the base and long enough to cover both the base and the ends of the tin. Press into place. Grease the paper all over.

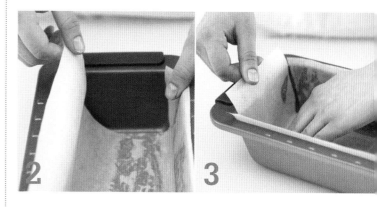

Bread and cakes

Baking presents the greatest challenge when cooking wheat-free, but even here most recipes can be adapted very easily.

Wheat-free baking

Wheat-free flours often have a different texture to wheat flour and take a bit of getting used to, but make very good substitutes. Some, for example maize, chestnut, buckwheat and gram (chickpea), have distinct flavours. Others, like rice and tapioca flours, are bland and are usually not suitable to be used on their own. Experiment to find which blend/combination works best for you. (See also page 17 for advice on lining tins when baking.)

Wheat-free flours tend to absorb more liquid. Be prepared to add a little extra liquid to achieve the right consistency for the recipe.

Gluten-free flours, available from supermarkets and health food shops, are usually suitable for wheat-free diets and can be substituted for wheat flour when making pastry, and baking cakes and biscuits.

When making cakes using proprietary gluten-free flours, allow 1 tsp wheat-free baking powder per 225g (8oz) flour.

Spelt flour (if you can tolerate it) can be substituted for brown and wholewheat flours.

Adding ground almonds, 25–50g (1–2oz), as part of the quantity of wheat-free flour required in a cake mix, adds a delicious touch of luxury to home-made cakes and helps keep the cake moist.

Maize (polenta) makes nutty, grainy cakes: use all polenta, or a mixture of polenta and gluten-free flour, or a mixture of polenta, ground nuts and gluten-free flour.

Chestnut flour (up to 10%) adds a deep richness to cakes; soya flour (up to 5%) makes a cake more nutritious. Both have strong flavours, so use small amounts.

A mixture of brown rice flour and tapioca flour makes good biscuits.

Substituting gluten-free flour with rice flour for half the quantity of flour required adds texture to cakes and biscuits.

Try using half rice flour and half buckwheat flour in your Christmas cake or rich fruit cakes. Rye flour also produces good results.

Corn breads are ideal for brunch. Use all maize flour or a mixture of maize flour and gram (chickpea) flour. Add extra flavours or a little sugar to mask the inherent bitterness of maize flour.

Gram (chickpea) flour makes extra-savoury cheese biscuits. Use up to 10%. A little chickpea flour can also be added to pastry mixes, and helps keep the pastry firm.

Try making your own oatcakes – it is easy to do.

Ground almonds/walnuts/hazelnuts make delicious macaroons.

Basic ingredients

Yeast Fresh yeast is activated when blended with warm liquid. Dried yeast needs sugar to activate it (no sugar is needed if using milk): blend the yeast with a little of the water plus sugar (or milk) and leave for 15 minutes to froth. Fast-action (easy-blend) dried yeast is sprinkled directly into the flour and the liquid added afterwards. As a rough guide, for 700g (1½lb) flour use 15g (½oz) fresh yeast, 1 tbsp dried yeast or a 7g sachet (2 tsp) fast-action dried yeast.

Liquid This needs to be slightly warm to the fingertips. Milk gives bread a softer texture than water.

Flour Brown or white gluten-free flour can be substituted for strong white or wholemeal bread flour in many recipes.

Salt This controls fermentation and adds flavour.

Fats Some recipes include fat for flavour and to improve keeping quality.

Cook's tips

Gluten-free breads are more cake-like in texture and taste but are still suitable for all recipes requiring bread. If you have a breadmaking machine, use this, following the manufacturer's instructions.

Cooling is important because if baked bread is left for too long either in the loaf tin or on the baking sheet, steam will gather and the underneath will become soggy. To prevent this, always remove the loaf immediately and put it on a wire rack. Then leave it to cool completely before slicing.

Seeded wheat-free loaf

You will need:
2 tsp fast-action (easy-blend) dried yeast, 2 tsp light muscovado sugar, 300g (11oz) gluten-free white bread flour, plus extra to dust, 200g (7oz) gluten-free brown bread flour, 1 tbsp each sunflower, linseed and poppy seeds, 1 tsp salt, 1 medium egg, lightly beaten.

1 Stir the yeast and sugar into 150ml (¼ pint) tepid water and leave to stand for 15 minutes until frothy. Lightly oil a 900g (2lb) loaf tin.

2 In a large bowl, beat together the flours, seeds, salt, yeast mixture, egg and a further 225ml (8fl oz) tepid water to make a soft, thick dough. Form the dough into an oblong shape and drop into the oiled loaf tin. Cover with lightly oiled clingfilm and leave to rise in a warm place for 45 minutes or until it reaches the top of the tin.

3 Preheat the oven to 200°C (180°C fan oven) mark 6. Slash the top of the loaf with a sharp knife and dust with flour.

4 Bake for 45–50 minutes or until the loaf sounds hollow when tapped underneath. Transfer to a wire rack and leave to cool..

Preparing long-grain rice

Long-grain rice needs no special preparation, although basmati should be washed to remove excess starch.

1   Put in a bowl and cover with cold water. Stir until this becomes cloudy, then drain and repeat the washing process until the water is clear.

2   Drain the rice before cooking.

Cooking rice and grains

There are two main types of rice: long-grain and short-grain. Long-grain rice is generally served as an accompaniment, while short-grain rice is used for dishes such as risotto, sushi and paella. Other grains, such as corn (ground to make polenta), quinoa and barley, can also be served as side dishes or in salads and pilafs.

Perfect rice

Use 50–75g (2–3oz) raw rice per person – or measure by volume: 50–75ml (2–2¹/₂fl oz).
If you cook a lot of rice, you may want to invest in a special rice steamer. They are available in Asian supermarkets and some kitchen shops and give good, consistent results.

Cooking long-grain rice

1 Measure the rice by volume and put it in a pan with a pinch of salt with twice the volume of boiling water (or boiling stock).

2 Bring to the boil. Turn the heat down to low, and set the timer for the time stated on the pack. The rice should be al dente: tender but with a hint of bite at the centre.

3 When the rice is cooked, fluff up the grains by gently tossing with a fork; this keeps the grains from sticking together. The rice can be left, covered, for a few minutes.

Variation

Cooking the rice in stock, with additional aromatics such as herbs, garlic or spices, will add flavour.

Basic risotto

Italian risotto is made with medium-grain arborio, vialone nano or carnaroli rice, which release starch to give a rich, creamy texture. It is traditionally cooked on the hob, but can also be cooked in the oven.

To serve four, you will need:

1 onion, chopped, 50g (2oz) butter, 900ml (1½ pints) hot chicken stock, 225g (8oz) risotto rice, 50g (2oz) freshly grated Parmesan, plus extra to serve.

1 Gently fry the onion in the butter for 10–15 minutes until it is very lightly coloured. Heat the stock in a pan and keep at a simmer. Add the rice to the butter and stir for 1–2 minutes until well coated.

2 Add a ladleful of stock and stir constantly until absorbed. Add the remaining stock a ladleful at a time, stirring, until the rice is al dente (tender but still with bite at the centre), about 20–30 minutes. **Note:** you may not need all the stock.

3 Stir in the grated Parmesan and serve immediately, with extra cheese passed separately.

Traditional polenta

1 Fill a pan with 1.1 litres (2 pints) water and add ¼ tsp salt. Pour in 225g (8oz) polenta and put it over the heat.

2 As the water starts to heat up, stir the polenta. Bring to the boil, reduce the heat to a simmer and continue cooking, stirring every few minutes, for 15–20 minutes until it comes away from the sides of the pan.

Cooking polenta

This classic Italian staple made of coarse ground cornmeal may be cooked to make a grainy purée to be served immediately, or cooled and then fried or grilled. Here are some quick ways to cook it.

Perfect polenta

Use coarse cornmeal if you want a slightly gritty texture, or fine cornmeal for a smooth texture.
If you are serving traditional polenta straight from the pan, have all the other dishes ready – the polenta needs to be eaten straightaway, otherwise it becomes thick and difficult to serve.

Grilling polenta

1 Make traditional polenta (see left), then pour into an oiled baking dish. Smooth the surface with a spatula and leave to cool.

2 Cut the polenta into squares and brush the pieces with olive oil.

3 Preheat the grill or frying pan and cook for 5–10 minutes until hot and browned on both sides.

Baking polenta

1 Preheat the oven to 200°C (180°C fan oven) mark 6. Fill a pan with 1.1 litres (2 pints) water and add ¼ tsp salt. Pour in 225g (8oz) polenta and put it over the heat. Bring to the boil, stirring, then simmer for 5 minutes.

2 Pour the polenta into an oiled baking dish, cover with foil and bake in the oven for 45–50 minutes. Brown under the grill.

Cooking other grains

Quinoa

This nutritious South American grain makes a great alternative to rice.

1 Put the quinoa in a bowl of cold water. Mix well, soak for 2 minutes, then drain. Put in a pan with twice its volume of water. Bring to the boil.

2 Simmer for 10–20 minutes, according to the packet instructions. Remove from the heat, cover and leave to stand for 10 minutes.

Quantities

Allow 50–75g (2–3oz) raw grain per person. Or, if measuring by volume, allow 50–75ml (2–2½fl oz).

Barley

There are three types of barley, all of which may be cooked on their own, or in a soup or stew.

Whole barley Soak the barley overnight in twice its volume of water, then drain well. Put the barley in a heavy-based pan, pour over boiling water and simmer for about 1½ hours or until tender. Check the liquid, adding more if necessary.

Scotch (pot) barley Rinse well, then simmer gently in boiling water for 45–50 minutes until tender.

Pearl barley This barley has had all of its outer husk removed, and needs no soaking. Rinse the barley and put it into a pan with twice its volume of water. Bring to the boil. Turn down the heat and simmer for 25–30 minutes until tender.

Cooking beans

1 Pick through the beans to remove any grit or small stones.

2 Put the beans in a bowl or pan and pour over cold water to cover generously. Leave to soak for at least 8 hours, then drain. (If you are in a hurry, pour over boiling water and leave the beans to cool in the water for 1–2 hours.)

3 Put the soaked beans in a large pan and add water to cover by at least 5cm (2in). Bring to the boil and boil rapidly for 10 minutes.

4 Skim off the scum that rises to the top, turn down the heat and leave to simmer until the beans are soft inside. They should be tender but not falling apart. Check the water periodically to make sure there's enough to keep the beans well covered. Drain well. If using in a salad, allow to cool completely.

Using beans and lentils

Many dried beans and peas need to be soaked overnight before cooking. However, lentils do not need soaking and are quicker to cook. Quicker still are canned beans: they are ready to use, but should be drained in a sieve and rinsed in cold water first.

Cooking times

Times vary for different dried beans, peas and lentils. Older beans will take longer to cook, so use them within their 'best before' date.

Chickpeas	1–2 hours
Red kidney, cannellini, borlotti, butter, flageolet beans	1–3 hours
Red lentils	20 minutes
Green lentils	30–40 minutes

Zesting citrus fruits

1   Wash and thoroughly dry the fruit. Using a vegetable peeler or a small sharp knife, cut away the zest (the coloured outer layer of skin), taking care to leave behind all the bitter white pith. Remove as much zest as you need.

2   Stack the slices of zest on a board and shred or dice as required.

Fruit basics

Nutritionally, fruit is important – both as a source of dietary fibre and of minerals and vitamins, especially vitamin C. Some varieties, especially apricots, mangoes and peaches, also provide vitamin A in the form of carotene. All fruits provide some energy, in the form of fructose (or fruit sugar), but most varieties are very low in fat and therefore low in calories. A few simple techniques can make preparing both familiar and not-so-familiar fruits quick and easy.

Segmenting citrus fruits

1   Cut off a slice at both ends of the fruit, then cut off the peel, just inside the white pith.

2   Hold the fruit over a bowl to catch the juice and cut between the segments just inside the membrane to release the flesh. Continue until all the segments are removed. Squeeze the juice from the membrane into the bowl and use as required.

Preparing pineapple

1 Cut off the base and crown of the pineapple, and stand the fruit on a chopping board.

2 Using a medium-sized knife, peel away a section of skin, going just deep enough to remove all or most of the hard, inedible 'eyes' on the skin. Repeat all the way around.

3 Use a small knife to cut out any remaining traces of the eyes.

4 Cut the peeled pineapple into slices.

5 You can buy special tools for coring pineapples but a 7.5cm (3in) biscuit cutter or an apple corer works just as well. Place the biscuit cutter directly over the core and press down firmly. If using an apple corer, cut out the core in pieces, as it will be too wide to remove in one piece.

Preparing mangoes

1 Cut a slice to one side of the stone in the centre. Repeat on the other side.

2 Cut parallel lines into the flesh of one slice, almost to the skin. Cut another set of lines to cut the flesh into squares.

3 Press on the skin side to turn the fruit inside out, so that the flesh is thrust outwards. Cut off the chunks as close as possible to the skin. Repeat with the other half.

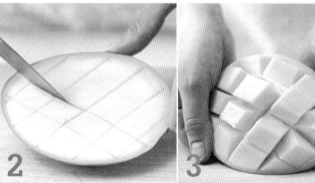

Preparing papaya

1 If using in a salad, peel the fruit using a swivel-headed vegetable peeler, then gently cut in half using a sharp knife. Remove the seeds using a teaspoon and slice the flesh, or cut into cubes.

2 If serving on its own, halve the fruit lengthways using a sharp knife, then use a teaspoon to scoop out the shiny black seeds and fibres inside the cavity.

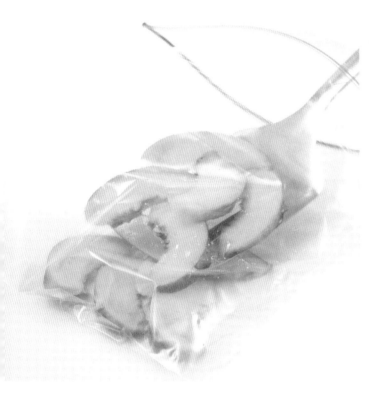

Food storage and hygiene

Storing food properly and preparing it in a hygienic way is important to ensure that food remains as nutritious and flavourful as possible, and to reduce the risk of food poisoning.

Hygiene

When you are preparing food, always follow these important guidelines:

Wash your hands thoroughly before handling food and again between handling different types of food, such as raw and cooked meat and poultry. If you have any cuts or grazes on your hands, be sure to keep them covered with a waterproof plaster.

Wash down worksurfaces regularly with a mild detergent solution or multi-surface cleaner.

Use a dishwasher if available. Otherwise, wear rubber gloves for washing-up, so that the water temperature can be hotter than unprotected hands can bear. Change drying-up cloths and cleaning cloths regularly. Note that leaving dishes to drain is more hygienic than drying them with a teatowel.

Keep raw and cooked foods separate, especially meat, fish and poultry. Wash kitchen utensils in between preparing raw and cooked foods. Never put cooked or ready-to-eat foods directly on to a surface which has just had raw fish, meat or poultry on it.

Keep pets out of the kitchen if possible; or make sure they stay away from worksurfaces. Never allow animals on to worksurfaces.

Shopping

Always choose fresh ingredients in prime condition from stores and markets that have a regular turnover of stock to ensure you buy the freshest produce possible.

Make sure items are within their 'best before' or 'use by' date. (Foods with a longer shelf life have a 'best before' date; more perishable items have a 'use by' date.)

Pack frozen and chilled items in an insulated cool bag at the check-out and put them into the freezer or refrigerator as soon as you get home.

During warm weather in particular, buy perishable foods just before you return home. When packing items at the check-out, sort them according to where you will store them when you get home – the refrigerator, freezer, storecupboard, vegetable rack, fruit bowl, etc. This will make unpacking easier – and quicker.

The storecupboard

Although storecupboard ingredients will generally last a long time, correct storage is important:

Always check packaging for storage advice – even with familiar foods, because storage requirements may change if additives, sugar or salt have been reduced. Check storecupboard foods for their 'best before' or 'use by' date and do not use them if the date has passed.

Keep all food cupboards scrupulously clean and make sure food containers and packets are properly sealed.

Once opened, treat canned foods as though fresh. Always transfer the contents to a clean container, cover and keep in the refrigerator. Similarly, jars, sauce bottles and cartons should be kept chilled after opening. (Check the label for safe storage times after opening.)

Transfer dry goods such as sugar, rice and pasta to moisture-proof containers. When supplies are used up, wash the container well and thoroughly dry before refilling with new supplies.

Store oils in a dark cupboard away from any heat source as heat and light can make them turn rancid and affect their colour. For the same reason, buy olive oil in dark green bottles.

Store vinegars in a cool place; they can turn bad in a warm environment.

Store dried herbs, spices and flavourings in a cool, dark cupboard or in dark jars. Buy in small quantities as their flavour will not last indefinitely.

Store flours and sugars in airtight containers.

Refrigerator storage

Fresh food needs to be kept in the cool temperature of the refrigerator to keep it in good condition and discourage the growth of harmful bacteria. Store day-to-day perishable items, such as opened jams and jellies, mayonnaise and bottled sauces, in the refrigerator along with eggs and dairy products, fruit juices, bacon, fresh and cooked meat (on separate shelves), and salads and vegetables (except potatoes, which don't suit being stored in the cold). A refrigerator should be kept at an operating temperature of 4–5°C.

It is worth investing in a refrigerator thermometer to ensure the correct temperature is maintained. To ensure your refrigerator is functioning effectively for safe food storage, follow these guidelines:

To avoid bacterial cross-contamination, store cooked and raw foods on separate shelves, putting cooked foods on the top shelf. Ensure that all items are well wrapped.

Never put hot food into the refrigerator, as this will cause the internal temperature of the refrigerator to rise.

Avoid overfilling the refrigerator, as this restricts the circulation of air and prevents the appliance from working properly.

It can take some time for the refrigerator to return to the correct operating temperature once the door has been opened, so don't leave it open any longer than is necessary.

Clean the refrigerator regularly, using a specially formulated germicidal refrigerator cleaner. Alternatively, use a weak solution of bicarbonate of soda: 1 tbsp to 1 litre (1¾ pints) water.

If your refrigerator doesn't have an automatic defrost facility, defrost regularly.

Maximum refrigerator storage times

For pre-packed foods, always adhere to the 'use by' date on the packet. For other foods the following storage times should apply, providing the food is in prime condition when it goes into the refrigerator and that your refrigerator is in good working order:

Vegetables and Fruit

Green vegetables	3–4 days
Salad leaves	2–3 days
Hard and stone fruit	3–7 days
Soft fruit	1–2 days

Dairy Food

Cheese, hard	1 week
Cheese, soft	2–3 days
Eggs	1 week
Milk	4–5 days

Fish

Fish	1 day
Shellfish	1 day

Raw Meat

Bacon	7 days
Game	2 days
Joints	3 days
Minced meat	1 day
Offal	1 day
Poultry	2 days
Raw sliced meat	2 days
Sausages	3 days

Cooked Meat

Joints	3 days
Casseroles/stews	2 days
Pies	2 days
Sliced meat	2 days
Ham	2 days
Ham, vacuum-packed (or according to the instructions on the packet)	1–2 weeks

1

Start the Day

Raspberry and Kiwi Smoothie

3 kiwi fruit

200g (7oz) raspberries

200–250ml (7–9fl oz) freshly squeezed orange juice

4 tbsp Greek yogurt

1 Peel and roughly chop the kiwi fruit and put into a blender with the raspberries, orange juice and yogurt. Blend until smooth, then serve.

Serves	EASY		NUTRITIONAL INFORMATION	
2	**Preparation Time** 8 minutes		**Per Serving** 140 calories, 4g fat (of which 2g saturates), 24g carbohydrate, 0.1g salt	Vegetarian Gluten free

Try Something Different

Use a mixture of raspberries, blackberries or chopped nectarines or peaches instead of the strawberries and blueberries.

25g (1oz) hazelnuts, roughly chopped

125g (4oz) rolled oats

1 tbsp olive oil

125g (4oz) strawberries, sliced

250g (9oz) blueberries

200g (7oz) Greek yogurt

2 tbsp runny honey

Toasted Oats with Berries

1 Preheat the grill to medium. Put the hazelnuts into a bowl with the oats. Drizzle with the olive oil, mix well, then spread out on a baking sheet. Toast the oat mixture for 5–10 minutes until it starts to crisp up. Remove from the heat and set aside to cool.

2 Put the strawberries into a large bowl with the blueberries and yogurt. Stir in the oats and hazelnuts, drizzle with the honey and divide among four dishes. Serve immediately.

EASY		NUTRITIONAL INFORMATION		Serves
Preparation Time 10 minutes, plus cooling	**Cooking Time** 5–10 minutes	**Per Serving** 327 calories, 15g fat (of which 3g saturates), 44g carbohydrate, 0.1g salt	Vegetarian	**4**

Cook's Tip

Put the apples, lemon juice, sugar and water into a microwave-safe bowl, cover loosely with clingfilm and cook on full power in a 850W microwave for 4 minutes until the apple is just soft.

Apple Compote

250g (9oz) cooking apples, peeled, cored and chopped

juice of ½ lemon

1 tbsp golden caster sugar

ground cinnamon

raisins, chopped almonds and natural yogurt to serve

1 Put the apples into a pan with the lemon juice, sugar and 2 tbsp cold water. Cook gently for 5 minutes until soft.

2 Sprinkle a little ground cinnamon over the top and chill. It will keep for up to three days.

3 Serve with the raisins, chopped almonds and yogurt.

Serves	EASY		NUTRITIONAL INFORMATION	
2	**Preparation Time** 10 minutes, plus chilling	**Cooking Time** 5 minutes	**Per Serving** 188 calories, 7g fat (of which 1g saturates), 29g carbohydrate, 0g salt	Vegetarian Gluten free • Dairy free

Try Something Different

Use chopped dried apricots, dried sour cherries or dried cranberries instead of the blueberries.

Blueberry Muffins

250g (9oz) wheat-free flour

2 tsp wheat-free baking powder

1 tsp bicarbonate of soda

125g (4oz) golden caster sugar

75g (3oz) ground almonds

finely grated zest of 1 lemon

125g (4oz) dried blueberries

1 medium egg

1 tsp vanilla extract

250ml (9fl oz) skimmed milk

50g (2oz) unsalted butter, melted

1 Preheat the oven to 200°C (180°C fan oven) mark 6. Line a muffin tin with 12 paper muffin cases.

2 Put the flour, baking powder and bicarbonate of soda into a bowl, then stir in the caster sugar, ground almonds, lemon zest and dried blueberries.

3 Put the egg, vanilla extract, milk and butter into a jug and mix together with a fork. Pour this liquid into the dry ingredients and lightly fold together.

4 Spoon the mixture into the muffin cases to three-quarters fill them and bake in the oven for 15 minutes or until the muffins are risen, pale golden and just firm.

5 Transfer the muffins to a wire rack and leave to cool slightly before serving.

EASY		NUTRITIONAL INFORMATION		Makes
Preparation Time 15 minutes	**Cooking Time** 15 minutes	**Per Muffin** 228 calories, 8g fat (of which 3g saturates), 36g carbohydrate, 0.1g salt	Vegetarian	**12**

Breakfast Bruschetta

1 ripe banana

250g (9oz) blueberries

200g (7oz) Quark

4 slices pumpernickel or
wheat-free wholegrain bread

1 tbsp runny honey

1 Slice the banana and put in a bowl with the blueberries. Spoon in the Quark and mix well.

2 Toast the slices of bread on both sides, then spread with the blueberry mixture. Drizzle with the honey

Serves	EASY		NUTRITIONAL INFORMATION	
4	**Preparation Time** 5 minutes	**Cooking Time** 5 minutes	**Per Serving** 145 calories, 1g fat (of which trace saturates), 30g carbohydrate, 0.4g salt	Vegetarian

Smoked Haddock Rarebit

4 x 150g (5oz) smoked haddock fillets, skinned

4 slices gluten-free bread

200g (7oz) spinach

2 large tomatoes

300g (11oz) low-fat crème fraîche

salt and ground black pepper

1 Preheat the grill. Season the haddock fillets and put into a shallow ovenproof dish. Grill for 6–8 minutes until opaque and cooked through.

2 Toast the bread on both sides until golden.

3 Wash the spinach, squeeze out the water and put in a pan. Cover and cook for 1-2 minutes until starting to wilt. Tip into a bowl. Slice the tomatoes.

4 Top each piece of toast with a piece of fish, then add the spinach and tomato slices. Spoon over the crème fraîche and grill for 2–3 minutes to heat through. Season with pepper and serve immediately.

Serves 4	EASY		NUTRITIONAL INFORMATION	
	Preparation Time 5 minutes	**Cooking Time** 10–15 minutes	**Per Serving** 481 calories, 32g fat (of which 21g saturates), 16g carbohydrate, 3.4g salt	Gluten free

▼ Rosti Potatoes with Fried Eggs
▶ *Lunch:* Creamy Watercress Soup
   (see page 48)
▶ *Supper:* Chickpeas with Spinach
   (see page 80)
▶ *Pudding:* Apple and Raspberry Mousse
   (see page 115)

Rösti Potatoes with Fried Eggs

900g (2lb) red potatoes, scrubbed and left whole

40g (1½oz) butter

4 large eggs

salt and ground black pepper

sprigs of flat-leafed parsley to garnish

1 Put the potatoes into a pan of cold water. Cover, bring to the boil and parboil for 5–8 minutes. Drain and leave to cool for 15 minutes.

2 Preheat the oven to 150°C (130°C fan oven) mark 2. Put a baking tray inside to warm. Peel the potatoes and coarsely grate them lengthways into long strands. Divide into eight portions and shape into mounds.

3 Melt half the butter in a large non-stick frying pan. When it is beginning to brown, add four of the potato mounds, spacing them well apart, and flatten them a little. Fry slowly for 6–7 minutes until golden brown, then turn them and brown the second side for 6–7 minutes. Transfer to a warmed baking tray and keep warm in the oven while you fry the rest.

4 Just before serving, carefully break the eggs into the hot pan and fry for about 2 minutes until the white is set and the yolk is still soft. Season with salt and pepper and serve at once, with the rösti. Garnish with sprigs of parsley.

EASY		NUTRITIONAL INFORMATION		Serves
Preparation Time 20 minutes, plus 15 minutes cooling	**Cooking Time** 20–25 minutes	**Per Serving** 324 calories, 16g fat (of which 7g saturates), 36g carbohydrate, 0.4g salt	Vegetarian Gluten free	**4**

Try Something Different

Blend 25g (1oz) mild goat's cheese with 1 tbsp crème fraîche; put in the centre of the omelette before folding.
Toss 25g (1oz) chopped smoked salmon or cooked smoked haddock with a little chopped dill and 1 tbsp crème fraîche; scatter over the omelette before folding.

Classic French Omelette

2–3 medium eggs

1 tbsp milk or water

25g (1oz) unsalted butter

salt and ground black pepper

sliced or grilled tomatoes and freshly chopped flat-leafed parsley to serve

1   Whisk the eggs in a bowl, just enough to break them down – overbeating spoils the texture of the omelette. Season with salt and pepper and add the milk or water.

2   Heat the butter in an 18cm (7in) omelette pan or non-stick frying pan until it is foaming, but not brown. Add the eggs and stir gently with a fork or wooden spatula, drawing the mixture from the sides to the centre as it sets and letting the liquid egg in the centre run to the sides. When set, stop stirring and cook for 30 seconds or until the omelette is golden brown underneath and still creamy on top; don't overcook. If you are making a filled omelette (see above), add the filling at this point.

3   Tilt the pan away from you slightly and use a palette knife to fold over one-third of the omelette to the centre, then fold over the opposite third. Slide the omelette out on to a warmed plate, letting it flip over so that the folded sides are underneath. Serve immediately, with tomatoes, sprinkled with parsley.

Serves 1	EASY		NUTRITIONAL INFORMATION	
	Preparation Time 5 minutes	**Cooking Time** 5 minutes	**Per Serving** 449 calories, 40g fat (of which 19g saturates), 1g carbohydrate, 1g salt	Vegetarian Gluten free • Dairy free

Try Something Different

For a more substantial meal, serve on wheat-free bread, such as 100% rye bread or German pumpernickel.

Poached Eggs with Mushrooms

8 medium-sized flat or Portobello mushrooms

40g (1½oz) butter

8 medium eggs

225g (8oz) baby spinach leaves

4 tsp fresh pesto

1　Preheat the oven to 200°C (180°C fan oven) mark 6. Arrange the mushrooms in a single layer in a small roasting tin and dot with the butter. Roast for 15 minutes until golden brown and soft.

2　Meanwhile, bring a wide shallow pan of water to the boil. When the mushrooms are half-cooked and the water is bubbling furiously, break the eggs into the pan, spaced well apart, then take the pan off the heat. The eggs will take about 6 minutes to cook.

3　When the mushrooms are tender, put them on a warmed plate, cover and return to the turned-off oven to keep warm.

4　Put the roasting tin over a medium heat on the hob and add the spinach. Cook, stirring, for about 30 seconds until the spinach has just started to wilt.

5　The eggs should be set by now, so divide the mushrooms among four plates and top with a little spinach, a poached egg and a teaspoonful of pesto.

EASY		NUTRITIONAL INFORMATION		Serves
Preparation Time 15 minutes	**Cooking Time** 20 minutes	**Per Serving** 276 calories, 23g fat (of which 9g saturates), 1g carbohydrate, 0.7g salt	Vegetarian Gluten free	**4**

2

Soups, Salads and Quick Bites

Freezing Tip

Freeze the soup in a sealed container at step 3 for up to three months.

To use, defrost in the fridge overnight. Reheat gently and simmer over a low heat for 5 minutes.

Beetroot Soup

1 tbsp olive oil

1 onion, finely chopped

750g (1lb 10oz) raw beetroot, peeled and cut into 1cm (½in) cubes

275g (10oz) potatoes, roughly chopped

2 litres (3½ pints) hot vegetable stock

juice of 1 lemon

4 tbsp soured cream

25g (1oz) mixed root vegetable crisps

salt and ground black pepper

2 tbsp chopped chives to garnish

1. Heat the oil in a large pan, add the onion and cook for 5 minutes. Add the vegetables and cook for a further 5 minutes.

2. Add the stock and lemon juice, then bring to the boil. Season with salt and pepper, reduce the heat and simmer, half-covered, for 25 minutes. Cool slightly, then whiz in a blender until smooth.

3. Cool half the soup, then freeze it. Pour the remainder into a clean pan and reheat gently. Divide the soup among four warmed bowls. Add 1 tbsp soured cream to each bowl, top with a few vegetable crisps and sprinkle the chopped chives on top to serve.

Serves 8	EASY		NUTRITIONAL INFORMATION	
	Preparation Time 15 minutes	**Cooking Time** 40–45 minutes	**Per Serving** 216 calories, 9g fat (of which 3g saturates), 31g carbohydrate, 1.5g salt	Vegetarian Gluten free

Roasted Tomato and Pepper Soup

1.4kg (3lb) full-flavoured ripe tomatoes

2 red peppers, cored, seeded and chopped

4 garlic cloves, crushed

3 small onions, thinly sliced

6 thyme sprigs

4 tbsp olive oil

4 tbsp Worcestershire sauce

4 tbsp vodka

6 tbsp double cream

salt and ground black pepper

oregano sprigs to serve

1 Preheat the oven to 200°C (180°C fan oven) mark 6. Discard any stalks from the tomatoes. Put the tomatoes into a large roasting tin with the peppers, garlic and onions. Scatter 6 thyme sprigs on top, drizzle with the olive oil and roast for 25 minutes. Turn the vegetables over and roast for a further 30–40 minutes until tender and slightly charred.

2 Put one-third of the vegetables into a blender or food processor with 300ml (½ pint) hot water. Add the Worcestershire sauce, vodka, and seasoning if needed. Whiz until smooth, then press through a sieve into a pan.

3 Whiz the remaining vegetables with 450ml (¾ pint) hot water, then sieve and add to the pan.

4 To serve, warm the soup thoroughly, stirring occasionally. Pour into warmed bowls, add 1 tbsp double cream to each, then drag a cocktail stick through the cream to create a swirl. Scatter a few oregano leaves over the top to finish.

EASY		NUTRITIONAL INFORMATION		Serves
Preparation Time 20 minutes	**Cooking Time** 1 hour	**Per Serving** 239 calories, 16g fat (of which 6g saturates), 15g carbohydrate, 0.4g salt	Gluten free	**6**

Cucumber, Yogurt and Mint Soup

1 cucumber, coarsely grated

500g (1lb 2oz) Greek yogurt

a generous handful of mint leaves, chopped

1 large garlic clove, crushed

125ml (4fl oz) cold water or light vegetable or chicken stock

salt and ground black pepper

6 ice cubes and mint sprigs to serve

1   Set aside 6 tbsp of the cucumber. Put the remainder into a large bowl with all the remaining ingredients for the soup and mix together. Chill until required.

2   Before serving, stir the soup, then taste and adjust the seasoning. Spoon the soup into six bowls and drop an ice cube, 1 tbsp of the reserved cucumber and a few mint sprigs into each bowl.

Health Tip

Raw garlic is a wonderful tonic for your health and is world-renowned for its curative and protective powers, including lowering blood pressure and cholesterol levels.
Fresh garlic has plump, juicy, mild cloves and is available from May throughout the summer. It is the classic form of garlic to use for making pesto, salsa verde, garlic mayonnaise and chilled soups.

EASY	NUTRITIONAL INFORMATION		Serves
Preparation Time 15 minutes, plus chilling	**Per Serving** 105 calories, 9g fat (of which 4g saturates), 3g carbohydrate, 0.5g salt	Vegetarian Gluten free	**6**

Try Something Different

Use spinach instead of watercress.

Creamy Watercress Soup

250g (9oz) watercress

50g (2oz) butter

1 onion, finely chopped

700g (1½lb) potatoes, cut into small pieces

900ml (1½ pints) milk

900ml (1½ pints) vegetable stock

6 tbsp single cream

salt and ground black pepper

Parmesan crisps (see page 65) to serve (optional)

1 Trim the watercress and discard coarse stalks. Reserve a few sprigs for the garnish and roughly chop the rest.

2 Melt the butter in a large pan, add the onion and cook gently for 8–10 minutes until soft. Add the potatoes and cook for 1 minute, then pour in the milk and stock and bring to the boil. Reduce the heat and cook for 15–20 minutes until tender.

3 Take the pan off the heat. Stir in the watercress, then transfer to a blender and blend in batches until smooth. Pour the soup back into a clean pan.

4 Add the cream and season to taste. Heat through and serve with Parmesan crisps if you like. Garnish with the reserved watercress sprigs.

Serves 6	EASY		NUTRITIONAL INFORMATION	
	Preparation Time 15 minutes	**Cooking Time** 30 minutes	**Per Serving** 251 calories, 13g fat (of which 8g saturates), 26g carbohydrate, 0.4g salt	Vegetarian Gluten free

Cook's Tip

Chillies vary enormously in strength, from quite mild to blisteringly hot, depending on the type of chilli and its ripeness. Taste a small piece first to check it's not too hot for you.

Be extremely careful when handling chillies not to touch or rub your eyes with your fingers, as they will sting. Wash knives immediately after handling chillies for the same reason. As a precaution, use rubber gloves when preparing them if you like.

Chicken Broth

1 tbsp olive oil

about 300g (11oz) boneless, skinless chicken thighs, cubed

3 garlic cloves, crushed

2 medium red chillies, seeded and finely diced (see Cook's Tip)

1 litre (1¾ pints) chicken stock

250g (9oz) each green beans, broccoli, sugarsnap peas and courgettes, chopped

50g (2oz) wheat-free pasta shapes or spaghetti, broken into short lengths

1 Heat the oil in a large pan, add the chicken, garlic and chilli and cook for 5–10 minutes or until the chicken is opaque all over.

2 Add the stock, bring to the boil, then add the vegetables and simmer for 5 minutes or until the chicken is cooked through.

3 Meanwhile, cook the pasta in a separate pan of salted boiling water until just cooked – about 5–10 minutes, depending on the type of pasta.

4 Drain the pasta, add to the broth, and serve immediately.

EASY		NUTRITIONAL INFORMATION		Serves
Preparation Time 30 minutes	**Cooking Time** 15 minutes	**Per Serving** 229 calories, 7g fat (of which 1g saturates), 16g carbohydrate, 1.2g salt	Dairy free	**4**

Try Something Different

Thinly sliced mushrooms, diced red pepper, cubes of tofu (not silken) or cooked broccoli or asparagus spears can all be added. Add to the salad just before serving, and mix well.

Japanese Noodle Salad

2 tbsp sesame seeds

200g (7oz) Japanese 100% wheat-free soba noodles

2–3 tbsp tamari (wheat-free Japanese soy sauce)

1 tbsp sesame oil

1 tbsp rice vinegar

salt

small bunch spring onions, finely sliced, to serve

1 Dry-fry the sesame seeds in a frying pan until golden. Set aside.

2 Cook the noodles in a pan of salted boiling water for 5 minutes or until tender but firm. Drain and cool under cold running water. Drain again and put into a bowl.

3 Add the toasted sesame seeds, tamari, sesame oil and vinegar and toss to coat the noodles. Chill until needed or for up to 24 hours. To serve, top with spring onions.

Serves 4	EASY		NUTRITIONAL INFORMATION	
	Preparation Time 2 minutes, plus chilling	**Cooking Time** 7 minutes	**Per Serving** 268 calories, 10g fat (of which 1g saturates), 39g carbohydrate, 2g salt	Vegetarian Gluten free • Dairy free

Try Something Different

Instead of the orange, try a pink grapefruit; scatter with pomegranate seeds for a healthy, colourful garnish.

Green and Orange Salad

1 orange

1 tsp olive oil

$\frac{1}{2}$ tsp white wine vinegar

$\frac{1}{4}$ avocado, sliced

1 Little Gem lettuce, leaves torn

handful of chopped chives

handful of watercress, washed and roughly chopped

2 tbsp low-fat cottage cheese or 75g (3oz) tuna in brine, drained, or 75g (3oz) roast chicken, or 75g (3oz) drained canned beans

salt and ground black pepper

1 Cut the rind and pith from the orange, then cut the flesh into slices or segments.

2 Put the oil and wine vinegar into a serving bowl and mix together. Add the sliced avocado, lettuce leaves, chives and watercress and toss together. Arrange the orange slices on top with the cottage cheese, tuna, roast chicken or beans, season and serve.

EASY	NUTRITIONAL INFORMATION		Serves
Preparation Time 10 minutes	**Per Serving** 177 calories, 10g fat (of which 2g saturates), 15g carbohydrate, 0.3g salt	Vegetarian Gluten free	**1**

Griddled Polenta with Gorgonzola Salad

2 tbsp olive oil, plus extra to grease
300ml (1/2 pint) semi-skimmed milk
10 sage leaves, roughly chopped
125g (4oz) quick-cook polenta
2 garlic cloves, crushed
25g (1oz) butter
100g (3 1/2 oz) salad leaves
125g (4oz) Gorgonzola cheese, cut into cubes
125g (4oz) each sunblush tomatoes and roasted red peppers
salt and ground black pepper

1 Lightly oil a 450g (1lb) loaf tin. Put the milk in a pan, then add the sage, 1 scant tsp salt and 300ml (1/2 pint) water and bring to the boil. Add the polenta to the pan in a thin, steady stream, stirring, to make a smooth paste.

2 Reduce the heat, add the garlic and cook for about 8 minutes, stirring occasionally. Add the oil, then season with pepper and stir well. Press into the prepared loaf tin, smooth the top and leave to cool for 45 minutes.

3 Once the polenta is cool, turn out on to a board and cut into eight slices.

4 Melt the butter in a griddle pan and fry the polenta slices on each side until golden.

5 Divide among four plates. Add the salad, Gorgonzola, sunblush tomatoes and peppers, and serve.

Serves 4	EASY		NUTRITIONAL INFORMATION	
	Preparation Time 20 minutes, plus 45 minutes cooling	Cooking Time 20 minutes	Per Serving 362 calories, 22g fat (of which 11g saturates), 28g carbohydrate, 1.1g salt	Vegetarian Gluten free

Try Something Different

For an even more nutritious salad, add a few pumpkin seeds or sunflower seeds, or a handful of sprouted seeds such as alfalfa, or chopped watercress.
For extra bite, add a little finely chopped red chilli; for extra sweetness, add some strips of red pepper.
For extra flavour, add some chopped coriander or torn basil leaves.

100g (3½oz) shredded roast chicken, skin discarded

1 carrot, chopped

1 celery stick, chopped

¼ cucumber, chopped

handful of ripe cherry tomatoes, chopped

1 tbsp hummus

¼ lemon to serve

Easy Chicken Salad

1 Put the chicken into a shallow bowl. Add the carrot, celery, cucumber and cherry tomatoes.

2 Top with the hummus and serve with lemon for squeezing over the salad.

Serves	EASY		NUTRITIONAL INFORMATION	
1	**Preparation Time** 10 minutes		**Per Serving** 323 calories, 18g fat (of which 5g saturates), 17g carbohydrate, 0.9g salt	Gluten free Dairy free

Try Something Different

Use smoked turkey or duck instead of smoked chicken.
For extra flavour, add 2 rosemary sprigs and 2 bay leaves when cooking the lentils, removing them when you drain the lentils.

Warm Lentil, Chicken and Broccoli Salad

125g (4oz) Puy lentils
225g (8oz) broccoli, chopped
1 large garlic clove, crushed
1 tsp English mustard powder
2 tbsp balsamic vinegar
4 tbsp olive oil
1 red onion, sliced into rings
350g (12oz) smoked chicken breast, shredded
salt

1   Cook the lentils according to the packet instructions. Blanch the broccoli in a pan of boiling water for 2 minutes. Drain, refresh and set aside.

2   Put the garlic into a bowl and use a wooden spoon to combine it with a pinch of salt until creamy, then whisk in the mustard, vinegar and 3 tbsp olive oil. Set aside.

3   Heat the remaining oil in a frying pan, add the onion and cook for 5 minutes until softened.

4   Add the chicken and broccoli and stir-fry for 1–2 minutes. Stir in the lentils and dressing and serve warm.

EASY		NUTRITIONAL INFORMATION		Serves
Preparation Time 20 minutes	**Cooking Time** 30 minutes	**Per Serving** 405 calories, 21g fat (of which 5g saturates), 17g carbohydrate, 3.1g salt	Gluten free Dairy free	**4**

▶ *Start the day:* Apple Compote
(see page 34)

▼ Mild Spiced Chicken and Quinoa

▶ *Supper:* Baked Eggs (see page 84)

▶ *Treat:* Chocolate Cherry Roll
(see page 121)

Mild Spiced Chicken and Quinoa

2 tbsp mango chutney

juice of ½ lemon

1 tbsp olive oil

2 tsp mild curry powder

1 tsp paprika

350g (12oz) skinless, boneless chicken breast, cut
into thick strips

200g (7oz) quinoa

1 cucumber, roughly chopped

½ bunch spring onions, sliced

60g (2oz) ready-to-eat dried apricots, sliced

2 tbsp chopped mint, basil or tarragon

1 Put the chutney, lemon juice, ½ tbsp oil, curry powder and paprika into a bowl and mix together. Add the chicken and toss to coat.

2 Cook the quinoa in boiling water for 10–12 minutes until tender (or according to the packet instructions). Drain thoroughly. Put into a bowl, then stir in the cucumber, spring onions, apricots, herbs and remaining oil.

3 Put the chicken and marinade into a pan and fry over a high heat for 2–3 minutes, then add 150ml (¼ pint) water. Bring to the boil, then simmer for 5 minutes or until the chicken is cooked. Serve with the quinoa.

Serves 4	EASY		NUTRITIONAL INFORMATION	
	Preparation Time 15 minutes	**Cooking Time** 20 minutes	**Per Serving** 268 calories, 3g fat (of which trace saturates), 37g carbohydrate, 0.4g salt	Gluten free Dairy free

Try Something Different

Use garlic-infused oil instead of the olive oil. Scatter with freshly chopped flat-leafed parsley and the finely chopped skin of one preserved lemon.

250g (9oz) quinoa

400ml (14fl oz) hot vegetable or chicken stock

4 spring onions, finely chopped

20g (³/₄oz) mint, finely chopped

25g (1oz) pinenuts, toasted

2 tbsp lemon juice

3 tbsp olive oil

salt and ground black pepper

kebabs, grilled poultry, fish or shellfish to serve

Quinoa with Mint Dressing

1 Cook the quinoa in a pan with the stock for 10–12 minutes until tender (or according to the packet instructions). Drain thoroughly and put into a bowl.

2 Add the spring onions and mint to the bowl with the toasted pinenuts, lemon juice and olive oil. Stir until well mixed and season lightly. Serve with kebabs, grilled poultry, fish or shellfish.

EASY		NUTRITIONAL INFORMATION		Serves
Preparation Time 15 minutes	**Cooking Time** 10–12 minutes	**Per Serving** 264 calories, 13g fat (of which 2g saturates), 33g carbohydrate, 0g salt	Vegetarian Gluten free • Dairy free	**4**

Tuna Salad

400g can mixed beans, drained and rinsed

125g (4oz) flaked tuna

$1/2$ cucumber, chopped

1 red onion, finely sliced

2 ripe tomatoes, chopped

2 celery sticks, chopped

handful of baby spinach leaves

1 tbsp olive oil

2 tsp red wine vinegar

salt and ground black pepper

1 Put the beans into a bowl and add the tuna, cucumber, red onion, tomatoes, celery and spinach.

2 Mix together the oil and vinegar, season with salt and pepper, then toss through the bean mix and serve.

▶ *Start the day:* **Raspberry and Kiwi Smoothie (see page 32)**

▶ *Start the day:* **Classic French Omelette (see page 40)**

▲ **Lunch: Tuna Salad**

▶ **Supper: Leek and Broccoli Bake (see page 83)**

▶ **Treat: Ginger-glazed Pineapple (see page 112)**

EASY	**NUTRITIONAL INFORMATION**		Serves
Preparation Time 10 minutes	**Per Serving** 313 calories, 8g fat (of which 1g saturates), 35g carbohydrate, 2.1g salt	Gluten free Dairy free	2

Try Something Different

For a more traditional Niçoise salad, replace the salmon with a 300g (11oz) fresh tuna steak, cooked and flaked, and use 250g (9oz) cooked green beans instead of the mixed beans. Scatter with chopped anchovy fillets and flat-leafed parsley.

Salmon Niçoise

4 eggs

400g can mixed beans, drained and rinsed

50g (2oz) pitted black olives

250g (9oz) cherry tomatoes, halved

large handful of mixed salad leaves

1 tbsp olive oil

juice of $\frac{1}{2}$ lemon

200g (7oz) cooked salmon flakes

salt and ground black pepper

1 Cook the eggs in a pan of simmering water for 6 minutes. Drain, then peel and cut into quarters.

2 Put the beans into a salad bowl with the olives, halved cherry tomatoes and mixed salad leaves. Add the oil and lemon juice, season with salt and pepper and toss together. Divide among four serving plates, add the egg and salmon and serve.

Serves 4	EASY		NUTRITIONAL INFORMATION	
	Preparation Time 15 minutes	**Cooking Time** 6 minutes	**Per Serving** 290 calories, 16g fat (of which 3g saturates), 16g carbohydrate, 1.7g salt	Gluten free Dairy free

Try Something Different

Use basil-infused oil and increase the amount of oil to 2 tbsp. Use pinenuts instead of almonds, drizzle with balsamic vinegar and scatter with basil leaves to serve.

Green Beans and Flaked Almonds

200g (7oz) green beans
1 tsp olive oil
25g (1oz) flaked almonds
½ lemon
grilled fish or chicken to serve

1 Bring a large pan of water to the boil. Add the green beans and cook for 4–5 minutes. Drain.

2 Meanwhile, heat the oil in a large frying pan. Add the almonds and cook for 1–2 minutes until golden. Turn off the heat, add the drained beans to the frying pan and toss. Squeeze over a little lemon juice just before serving. Serve with grilled fish or chicken.

EASY		NUTRITIONAL INFORMATION		Serves
Preparation Time 5 minutes	**Cooking Time** 5–7 minutes	**Per Serving** 57 calories, 5g fat (of which trace saturates), 2g carbohydrate, 0g salt	Vegetarian Gluten free • Dairy free	**4**

Egg and Pepper Pizza

150g (5oz) red and yellow marinated peppers in oil

8 tbsp passata

4 small wheat-free pizza bases

4 medium eggs

125g (4oz) watercress, washed and stalks removed

1 Preheat the oven to 220°C (200°C fan oven) mark 7 and preheat two large baking sheets, big enough to hold two pizzas each.

2 Drain the peppers, reserving the oil. Chop into thin strips. Spoon 2 tbsp passata over each pizza base and scatter strips of pepper around the edges. Make a dip in the passata in the middle of each pizza and break an egg into it. Carefully slide the pizzas on to the preheated baking sheets. Place in the oven and cook for 12 minutes until the egg is thoroughly cooked.

3 Top the pizzas with the watercress, drizzle with a little of the reserved oil from the peppers and serve.

Health Tip

Watercress is the salad superfood par excellence. It has been shown to have anti-cancer and health-enhancing properties, and is a good source of iron, and vitamins C and E.

	EASY		NUTRITIONAL INFORMATION	
Serves	**Preparation Time**	**Cooking Time**	**Per Serving**	
4	15 minutes	12 minutes	403 calories, 13g fat (of which 2g saturates), 61g carbohydrate, 1g salt	Vegetarian Gluten free

Tomato Salsa

4 large ripe tomatoes

1 large ripe avocado

2 tbsp freshly chopped coriander

juice of 1 lime

2 tbsp olive oil

salt and ground black pepper

barbecued or grilled chicken or fish, baked potatoes or green salad to serve

1 Cut the tomatoes into quarters and scoop out the seeds. Roughly chop the flesh and put into a bowl.

2 Slice the avocado in half, remove the stone and scoop out the flesh with a spoon. Chop and add to the tomato with the chopped coriander. Stir in the lime juice and oil. Season with salt and pepper.

3 Serve with barbecued or grilled chicken or fish, or baked potatoes. Alternatively, spoon the salsa over a green salad.

Serves 4	EASY	NUTRITIONAL INFORMATION	
	Preparation Time 15 minutes	**Per Serving** 142 calories, 13g fat (of which 2g saturates), 4g carbohydrate, 0g salt	Vegetarian Gluten free • Dairy free

Parmesan Crisps

125g (4oz) freshly grated Parmesan

1/2 tsp poppy seeds

1 Preheat the oven to 200°C (180°C fan oven) mark 6 and line two baking sheets with baking parchment. Evenly space heaped tablespoons of Parmesan on the sheets and spread each one out slightly. Sprinkle with poppy seeds and bake for 5–10 minutes until lacy and golden.

2 Leave on the tray for 2–3 minutes to cool and firm up slightly, then transfer to a wire rack. Serve as cocktail nibbles or to garnish soups, salads or pasta.

EASY		NUTRITIONAL INFORMATION		Serves
Preparation Time 5 minutes, plus 2–3 minutes cooling	**Cooking Time** 5–10 minutes	**Per Serving** 73 calories, 5g fat (of which 3g saturates), 0g carbohydrate, 0.4g salt	Vegetarian Gluten free	**8**

3

Easy Suppers

► *Start the day:* Breakfast Bruschetta (see page 36)

► Beetroot Soup (see page 44)

▼ *Supper:* Garlic Pork

► *Treat:* Griddled Peaches (see page 116)

Garlic Pork

1 tbsp olive oil

2 garlic cloves, crushed

5cm (2in) piece fresh root ginger, peeled and grated

4 pork chops

salt

stir-fried shredded cabbage to serve

1. Preheat the grill to high. Put the oil into a small bowl, add the garlic and ginger and a pinch of salt, and stir well to mix.

2. Grill the pork chops for 7–10 minutes on each side, then remove from the grill. Brush the oil mixture all over the chops, then return to the grill and cook for a further 2 minutes on each side. Serve with stir-fried shredded cabbage.

	EASY		NUTRITIONAL INFORMATION	
Serves **4**	**Preparation Time** 5 minutes	**Cooking Time** 20–25 minutes	**Per Serving** 181 calories, 8g fat (of which 2g saturates), 1g carbohydrate, 0.2g salt	Gluten free Dairy free

Try Something Different

Use pork fillet instead of beef, trimmed of fat and cut into thin slices.

1 tsp chilli oil

1 tbsp each tamari (wheat-free Japanese soy sauce) and runny honey

1 garlic clove, crushed

1 large red chilli, halved, seeded and chopped (see page 49)

400g (14oz) lean beef, cut into strips

1 tsp sunflower oil

1 broccoli head, thinly sliced

200g (7oz) mangetouts, halved

1 red pepper, halved, seeded and cut into strips

rice to serve

Sweet Chilli Beef Stir-fry

1 Pour the chilli oil into a medium-sized shallow bowl. Add the tamari, honey, garlic and chilli and stir well. Add the strips of beef and toss in the marinade.

2 Heat the sunflower oil in a wok over a high heat until it is very hot. Cook the strips of beef in two batches, for 3–4 minutes, or until just cooked through, then remove them from the wok and set aside. Wipe the wok with kitchen paper to remove any residue.

3 Add the broccoli, mangetouts, red pepper and 2 tbsp water and stir-fry for 5–6 minutes until starting to soften. Return the beef to the wok to heat through. Serve with rice.

EASY		NUTRITIONAL INFORMATION		Serves
Preparation Time 10 minutes	**Cooking Time** 10–15 minutes	**Per Serving** 273 calories, 13g fat (of which 5g saturates), 8g carbohydrate, 0.2g salt	Gluten free Dairy free	4

Ginger, Leek and Prawn Stir-fry

2 tsp olive oil

1 bunch spring onions, chopped

1 garlic clove, crushed

2.5cm (1in) piece fresh root ginger, peeled and grated

3 leeks, roughly chopped

1 red pepper, halved, seeded and roughly chopped

400g (14oz) cooked prawns

1 tbsp tamari (wheat-free Japanese soy sauce)

2 tsp tomato purée, diluted in 1 tbsp water

1 tsp runny honey

ground black pepper

rice or quinoa to serve

1 Heat the oil in a pan, add the spring onions, garlic, ginger and 2 tbsp water and fry for 2 minutes over a medium heat. Add the leeks and red pepper and stir-fry for 10 minutes until softened.

2 Add the prawns, tamari, tomato purée and honey to the pan. Season with pepper and cook for 30 seconds to 1 minute, stirring. Serve with rice or quinoa.

Try Something Different

Use scallops instead of the prawns. Alternatively use any firm-textured white fish such as monkfish, discarding the skin and cutting into small cubes.

EASY		NUTRITIONAL INFORMATION		Serves
Preparation Time 10 minutes	**Cooking Time** 15 minutes	**Per Serving** 152 calories, 3g fat (of which 1g saturates), 10g carbohydrate, 1.2g salt	Gluten free Dairy free	4

Health Tip

Oily fish such as sardines are one of the best sources of essential heart-protecting omega-3 oils. Eat them at least once a week. Fresh Cornish sardines, when they are available, are a treat and are cheap. Look out for them at your fishmongers or on the fresh fish counter at the supermarket.

Grilled Sardines with Harissa

1 garlic clove, crushed

2 tbsp olive oil

1–2 tsp harissa

4 whole sardines

salt and ground black pepper

tomato salad, watercress and lime wedges to serve

1 Preheat the grill to high. Put the garlic in a bowl. Add the oil and harissa, season to taste with salt and pepper, and mix together.

2 Slash the sardines a couple of times on each side, then brush the harissa and oil mixture all over. Grill for 5–10 minutes on each side until cooked through.

3 Serve with tomato salad, watercress and lime wedges to squeeze over the sardines.

Serves 2	EASY		NUTRITIONAL INFORMATION	
	Preparation Time 10 minutes	**Cooking Time** 10–20 minutes	**Per Serving** 292 calories, 21g fat (of which 4g saturates), 2g carbohydrate, 0.3g salt	Gluten free Dairy free

Try Something Different

Use another white fish such as sea bass or tilapia fillets instead of the cod.

Cod with Cherry Tomatoes

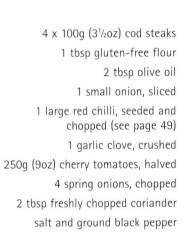

4 x 100g (3½oz) cod steaks

1 tbsp gluten-free flour

2 tbsp olive oil

1 small onion, sliced

1 large red chilli, seeded and chopped (see page 49)

1 garlic clove, crushed

250g (9oz) cherry tomatoes, halved

4 spring onions, chopped

2 tbsp freshly chopped coriander

salt and ground black pepper

1   Season the cod with salt and pepper, then lightly dust with the flour. Heat 1 tbsp oil in a large frying pan, add the onion and fry for 5–10 minutes until golden.

2   Pour the remaining oil into the pan. Add the cod and fry for 3 minutes on each side. Add the chilli, garlic, cherry tomatoes, spring onions and coriander, and season with salt and pepper. Cover and continue to cook for 5–10 minutes until everything is heated through. Serve immediately.

EASY		NUTRITIONAL INFORMATION		Serves
Preparation Time 15 minutes	**Cooking Time** 20–25 minutes	**Per Serving** 168 calories, 7g fat (of which 1g saturates), 8g carbohydrate, 0.2g salt	Gluten free Dairy free	**4**

Try Something Different

Use **swordfish** instead of tuna.

Peppered Tuna with Olive and Herb Salsa

1 tsp olive oil

zest and juice of 1 lime

1 tbsp cracked mixed peppercorns

4 x 150g (5oz) tuna steaks

For the olive and herb salsa

1 tbsp extra virgin olive oil

1 tbsp each black and green olives, roughly chopped

zest and juice of ½ lemon

2 tbsp freshly chopped parsley

1 tbsp freshly chopped coriander

1 tbsp capers, roughly chopped

salt and ground black pepper

1 Put the olive oil into a large, shallow bowl, then add the lime zest and juice and peppercorns. Add the tuna and turn to coat in the oil.

2 Heat a non-stick griddle pan until hot. Cook the tuna steaks, two at a time, for 2–3 minutes on each side.

3 Meanwhile, put all the ingredients for the salsa in a bowl and mix together. Season to taste and mix well, then serve with the tuna.

Serves 4	EASY		NUTRITIONAL INFORMATION	
	Preparation Time 15 minutes	**Cooking Time** 8–12 minutes	**Per Serving** 398 calories, 32g fat (of which 12g saturates), 1g carbohydrate, 1.9g salt	Gluten free Dairy free

▶ *Start the day:* **Poached Eggs with Mushrooms (see page 41)**

▶ *Lunch:* **Easy Chicken Salad (see page 54)**

▼ Plaice with Herb and Polenta Crust

Plaice with Herb and Polenta Crust

1 tsp finely chopped rosemary or 1 tsp finely snipped chives

1 tsp finely chopped thyme

2 garlic cloves, very finely chopped

50g (2oz) polenta

finely grated zest and juice of 2 small lemons

2 plaice fillets, about 175g (6oz) each, skinned

1 large egg

2 tbsp olive oil

salt and ground black pepper

roasted tomatoes, green beans and lemon wedges to serve

1 Combine the herbs, garlic and polenta on a flat plate. Add the lemon zest, salt and pepper and mix well. Wipe the plaice fillets with kitchen paper.

2 Beat the egg in a shallow dish, dip the fish fillets in the egg and coat them with the polenta mixture, pressing it on well.

3 Heat the oil in a very large frying pan over a high heat. When hot, add the fish, turn the heat down to medium and cook for about 2–3 minutes on each side, depending on the thickness of the fillets. Drain on kitchen paper. Serve with lemon juice poured over them, with roasted tomatoes, green beans and extra lemon wedges.

EASY		NUTRITIONAL INFORMATION		Serves
Preparation Time 15 minutes	**Cooking Time** 4–6 minutes	**Per Serving** 376 calories, 17g fat (of which 3g saturates), 19g carbohydrate, 0.6g salt	Gluten free Dairy free	**2**

Calf's Liver with Fried Sage and Balsamic Vinegar

15g (½ oz) butter plus a little olive oil for frying

12 sage leaves

4 thin slices of calf's liver

1–2 tbsp balsamic vinegar

rice, with freshly chopped parsley stirred through, or grilled polenta to serve

1 Melt the butter with a little olive oil in a heavy-based frying pan, and when hot add the sage leaves. Cook briefly for 1 minute or so until crisp. Remove, put in a single layer in a shallow dish and keep hot in the oven.

2 Add a little extra oil to the pan, put in two slices of calf's liver and cook quickly for 30 seconds on each side over a high heat. Remove and place on a plate while you quickly cook the remaining two slices.

3 Return all four slices to the pan, splash the balsamic vinegar over the top and cook for another minute or so.

4 Serve immediately with rice or grilled polenta.

▶ *Start the day:* Toasted Oats with Berries (see page 33)
▶ *Lunch:* Green and Orange Salad (see page 51)
▲ Calf's Liver with Fried Sage and Balsamic Vinegar
▶ *Treat:* Sticky Lemon Polenta Cake (see page 125)

Serves 4	EASY		NUTRITIONAL INFORMATION	
	Preparation Time 5 minutes	Cooking Time 5 minutes	Per Serving 88 calories, 6g fat (of which 3g saturates), trace carbohydrate, 0.1g salt	Gluten free Dairy free

Try Something Different

To use leftover chicken or turkey, don't fry the meat at step 2. Add it to the pan with the crème fraîche at step 3. Cook the leeks in 2 tsp olive oil.
For a different flavour, make the mash with 2 large potatoes and a small celeriac, peeled, cut into chunks and cooked with the potato.

5 large potatoes, peeled and chopped into chunks

200g (7oz) crème fraîche

3 chicken breasts with skin

3 large leeks, chopped into chunks

about 10 tarragon leaves, finely chopped

salt and ground black pepper

Chicken and Leek Pie

1 Preheat the oven to 200°C (180°C fan oven) mark 6. Put the potatoes into a pan of salted cold water. Cover, bring to the boil and simmer for 10–12 minutes until soft. Drain and return to the pan. Add 1 tbsp crème fraîche, season with salt and pepper, and mash well.

2 Meanwhile, heat a frying pan, add the chicken, skin-side down, and fry gently for 5 minutes until the skin is golden. Turn the chicken over and fry for 6–8 minutes. Remove the chicken from the pan and put on a board. Tip the leeks into the pan and cook in the juices over a low heat for 5 minutes to soften.

3 Discard the chicken skin and cut the flesh into bite-sized pieces (don't worry if it is not quite cooked through). Return the chicken to the pan, stir in the remaining crème fraîche and heat for 2–3 minutes until bubbling. Stir in the tarragon and season, then spoon into a 1.7 litre (3 pint) ovenproof dish. Spread the mash on top and cook in the oven for 20–25 minutes until golden and heated through.

Serves 4	EASY		NUTRITIONAL INFORMATION	
	Preparation Time 15 minutes	**Cooking Time** 40–45 minutes	**Per Serving** 591 calories, 23g fat (of which 15g saturates), 54g carbohydrate, 0.3g salt	Gluten free

Try Something Different

Instead of chicken use 700g (1½lb) lean lamb fillet or leg of lamb, cut into chunks.

Moroccan Spiced Chicken Kebabs

2 tbsp olive oil

15g (½oz) flat-leafed parsley

1 garlic clove

½ tsp paprika

1 tsp ground cumin

zest and juice of 1 lemon

4 skinless chicken breasts, cut into bite-sized chunks

salt

shredded lettuce, sliced cucumber and tomatoes, and lime wedges to serve

1 Put the oil into a blender and add the parsley, garlic, paprika, cumin, lemon zest and juice, and a pinch of salt. Whiz to make a paste.

2 Put the chicken into a medium-sized shallow dish and rub in the spice paste. Leave to marinate for at least 20 minutes. Preheat the grill to high.

3 Thread the marinated chicken on to soaked wooden skewers and grill for 10–12 minutes, turning every now and then, until the meat is cooked through. Serve with shredded lettuce, sliced cucumber and tomatoes, and lime wedges.

EASY		NUTRITIONAL INFORMATION		Serves
Preparation Time 10 minutes, plus marinating	**Cooking Time** 10–12 minutes	**Per Serving** 190 calories, 7g fat (of which 1g saturates), 1g carbohydrate, 0.2g salt	Gluten free Dairy free	**4**

Chickpeas with Spinach

3 tbsp olive oil

2.5cm (1in) piece fresh root ginger, peeled and finely chopped

3 garlic cloves, chopped

2 tsp each ground coriander and paprika

1 tsp ground cumin

2 x 400g cans chickpeas, drained and rinsed

4 tomatoes, roughly chopped

handful of coriander leaves

450g (1lb) fresh spinach

salt and ground black pepper

rice and grated carrots with lemon juice to serve

1 Heat the oil in a large, heavy-based pan, add the ginger, garlic and spices and cook for 2 minutes, stirring. Stir the chickpeas into the spices.

2 Add the tomatoes to the pan with the coriander leaves and spinach. Cook gently for 10 minutes. Season to taste with salt and pepper and serve immediately, with rice and a salad of grated carrots tossed in a little lemon juice.

Serves	EASY		NUTRITIONAL INFORMATION	
6	**Preparation Time** 10 minutes	**Cooking Time** 12–15 minutes	**Per Serving** 204 calories, 10g fat (of which 1g saturates), 21g carbohydrate, 0.8g salt	Vegetarian Gluten free • Dairy free

Baked Anchovy Potatoes and Parsnips

3 tbsp olive oil

450ml (¾ pint) hot vegetable or chicken stock

1 tbsp Dijon mustard

450g (1lb) each potatoes and parsnips, peeled and cut into bite-sized chunks

1 small onion, finely sliced

1 garlic clove, crushed

50g (2oz) canned anchovies in oil, drained and chopped

small handful of flat-leafed parsley, chopped

ground black pepper

roast chicken or grilled lamb and spinach to serve

1 Preheat the oven to 190°C (170°C fan oven) mark 5. Grease a 2 litre (3½ pint) ovenproof dish with 1 tbsp olive oil.

2 Pour the stock into a pan, add the mustard and bring to the boil. Add the potatoes and parsnips, return to the boil then remove from the heat. Season with pepper.

3 Heat 2 tbsp olive oil in a frying pan, add the onion and cook gently for 10 minutes until softened. Add the garlic to the onion and cook for 1–2 minutes, then remove from the heat and add the anchovies.

4 Put half the potatoes, parsnips and stock into the ovenproof dish, spoon over the onion and anchovy mixture over it, then cover with the remaining potatoes, parsnips and stock.

5 Cook, uncovered, in the oven for 1 hour or until tender and golden. Sprinkle the parsley over just before serving. Serve with roast chicken or grilled lamb and freshly cooked spinach.

EASY		NUTRITIONAL INFORMATION		Serves
Preparation Time 5 minutes	**Cooking Time** 20 minutes	**Per Serving** 187 calories, 8g fat (of which 1g saturates), 26g carbohydrate, 1g salt	Gluten free Dairy free	**6**

Leek and Broccoli Bake

2 tbsp olive oil

1 large red onion, cut into wedges

1 aubergine, chopped

2 leeks, cut into chunks

1 broccoli head, cut into florets and stalks chopped

3 large flat mushrooms, chopped

2 x 400g cans cherry tomatoes

3 rosemary sprigs, chopped

50g (2oz) Parmesan, freshly grated

salt and ground black pepper

1 Preheat the oven to 200°C (180°C fan oven) mark 6. Heat the oil in a large flameproof dish, add the onion, aubergine and leeks and cook for 10–12 minutes until golden and softened.

2 Add the broccoli, mushrooms, cherry tomatoes, half the rosemary and 300ml (½ pint) boiling water. Season with salt and pepper. Stir well, then cover and cook in the oven for 30 minutes.

3 Meanwhile, put the Parmesan into a bowl. Add the remaining rosemary and season with pepper. When the vegetables are cooked, remove the lid and sprinkle the Parmesan mixture on top. Cook, uncovered, in the oven for a further 5–10 minutes until the topping is golden.

Try Something Different

Use sliced courgettes instead of aubergine.

EASY		NUTRITIONAL INFORMATION		Serves
Preparation Time 20 minutes	**Cooking Time** 45–55 minutes	**Per Serving** 245 calories, 13g fat (of which 4g saturates), 18g carbohydrate, 0.4g salt	Vegetarian Gluten free	**4**

Baked Eggs

2 tbsp olive oil

125g (4oz) mushrooms, chopped

225g (8oz) fresh spinach

2 eggs

2 tbsp single cream

salt and ground black pepper

1 Preheat the oven to 200°C (180°C fan oven) mark 6. Heat the oil in a large frying pan, add the chopped mushrooms and stir-fry for 30 seconds. Add the spinach and stir-fry until wilted. Season to taste, then divide the mixture between two shallow ovenproof dishes.

2 Carefully break an egg into the centre of each dish, then spoon 1 tbsp single cream over each.

3 Cook in the oven for about 12 minutes until just set – the eggs will continue to cook a little once they're out of the oven. Grind a little more pepper over the top, if liked, and serve.

Serves	EASY		NUTRITIONAL INFORMATION	
2	**Preparation Time** 10 minutes	**Cooking Time** 15 minutes	**Per Serving** 238 calories, 21g fat (of which 5g saturates), 2g carbohydrate, 0.6g salt	Vegetarian Gluten free

▶ *Start the day:* Blueberry Muffins
(see page 35)
▶ *Lunch:* Courgette and Parmesan Frittata
(see page 89)
▼ Asparagus Risotto
▶ *Treat:* Exotic Fruit Salad (see page 117)

Asparagus Risotto

50g (2oz) butter

2 shallots, diced

2 garlic cloves, crushed

225g (8oz) arborio (risotto) rice

500ml (18fl oz) hot vegetable or chicken stock

2 tbsp mascarpone cheese

50g (2oz) Parmesan, finely grated, plus
shavings to garnish

2 tbsp freshly chopped parsley

400g (14oz) asparagus spears, blanched and halved

1 Melt the butter in a heavy-based pan, add the shallots and garlic, and sauté over a gentle heat until soft.

2 Stir in the rice, cook for 1–2 minutes, then add the stock. Bring to the boil and simmer for 15–20 minutes, stirring occasionally to ensure that the rice isn't sticking, until almost all the stock has been absorbed and the rice is tender.

3 Add the mascarpone, half the Parmesan and half the parsley to the pan. Stir in the asparagus and the remaining parsley and Parmesan. Divide among four plates, garnish with shavings of Parmesan and serve.

EASY		NUTRITIONAL INFORMATION		Serves
Preparation Time 10 minutes	**Cooking Time** 25 minutes	**Per Serving** 374 calories, 16g fat (of which 10g saturates), 47g carbohydrate, 1.1g salt	Vegetarian Gluten free	**4**

Stuffed Peppers

225g (8oz) brown basmati rice

1 tbsp olive oil

2 onions, chopped

400g can cherry tomatoes

3 tbsp freshly chopped coriander, plus extra sprigs to garnish

4 red peppers, halved and seeded, leaving stalks intact

150ml (¼ pint) hot vegetable stock

1 Preheat the oven to 200°C (180°C fan oven) mark 6. Cook the rice according to the packet instructions, then drain.

2 Meanwhile, heat the oil in a pan, add the onions and fry for 15 minutes. Add the tomatoes and leave to simmer for 10 minutes. Stir in the cooked rice and coriander, then spoon the mixture into the halved peppers.

3 Put the peppers into a roasting tin and pour the stock around them. Cook in the oven for 30 minutes until tender. Serve sprinkled with coriander sprigs.

Try Something Different

Add 25g (1oz) pinenuts or chopped cashew nuts to the cooked rice and coriander at step 2.

Serves	EASY		NUTRITIONAL INFORMATION	
4	**Preparation Time** 15 minutes	**Cooking Time** 55 minutes	**Per Serving** 208 calories, 5g fat (of which 1g saturates), 39g carbohydrate, 0g salt	Vegetarian Gluten free • Dairy free

Smoked Sesame Tofu

2 tbsp toasted sesame seeds

2 tbsp tamari (wheat-free Japanese soy sauce)

1 tsp light muscovado sugar

1 tsp rice wine vinegar

1 tbsp sesame oil

225g (8oz) smoked tofu, cubed

½ small white or green cabbage, shredded

2 carrots, cut into strips

200g (7oz) bean sprouts

4 roasted red peppers, roughly chopped

2 spring onions, shredded

brown rice to serve

1 Put the sesame seeds into a bowl, add the tamari, sugar, vinegar and ½ tbsp sesame oil. Mix together, then add the smoked tofu and stir to coat. Set aside to marinate for 10 minutes.

2 Heat a large wok or non-stick frying pan, add the marinated tofu, reserving the marinade, and fry for 5 minutes until golden all over. Remove from the wok with a slotted spoon and set aside.

3 Heat the remaining oil in the wok, add the cabbage and carrots and stir-fry for 5 minutes. Stir in the bean sprouts, peppers, spring onions, cooked tofu and reserved marinade and cook for a further 2 minutes. Serve immediately, with brown rice.

Serves 4	EASY		NUTRITIONAL INFORMATION	
	Preparation Time 20 minutes, plus 10 minutes marinating	**Cooking Time** 12 minutes	**Per Serving** 208 calories, 11g fat (of which 2g saturates), 19g carbohydrate, 1.4g salt	Vegetarian Gluten free • Dairy free

Try Something Different

Cherry tomato and rocket frittata: replace the courgettes with 175g (6oz) ripe cherry tomatoes, frying them for 1 minute only, until they begin to soften. Immediately after pouring in the eggs, scatter 25g (1oz) rocket leaves over the surface. Continue cooking as in step 3.

Courgette and Parmesan Frittata

40g (1½oz) butter

1 small onion, finely chopped

225g (8oz) courgettes, trimmed and finely sliced

6 medium eggs, beaten

25g (1oz) Parmesan, freshly grated, plus shavings to garnish

salt and ground black pepper

1 Melt 25g (1oz) butter in an 18cm (7in) non-stick frying pan and cook the onion for about 10 minutes until softened. Add the courgettes and fry gently for 5 minutes or until they begin to soften.

2 Beat the eggs in a bowl and season with salt and pepper.

3 Add the remaining butter to the pan and heat, then pour in the eggs. Cook for 2–3 minutes or until golden underneath and cooked around the edges. Meanwhile, preheat the grill to medium.

4 Sprinkle the grated cheese over the frittata and grill for 1–2 minutes until just set. Scatter with Parmesan shavings, cut into quarters and serve with a green salad.

EASY		NUTRITIONAL INFORMATION		Serves
Preparation Time 10 minutes	**Cooking Time** 15–20 minutes	**Per Serving** 229 calories, 19g fat (of which 9g saturates), 2g carbohydrate, 0.6g salt	Vegetarian Gluten free	4

4

Food for Friends

Try Something Different

Replace the trout with 225g (8oz) cooked salmon, haddock or smoked haddock. Skin, flake and add at stage 2.

Trout and Dill Fishcakes

4 medium potatoes, peeled and chopped

2 trout fillets

3 spring onions, finely chopped

2 dill sprigs, finely chopped

zest of 1 lemon

1 tbsp olive oil

a little plain gluten-free flour

salt

watercress to serve

1 Cook the potatoes in a pan of salted boiling water for 6–8 minutes until tender. Drain, return to the pan and mash.

2 Preheat the grill to high. Grill the trout fillets for 8–10 minutes until cooked through and firm to the touch. Skin the fish, flake into pieces, removing any bones, then put into the pan with the mashed potato.

3 Add the spring onions, dill and lemon zest to the pan with the olive oil, season with salt and mix together well.

4 Shape the mixture into eight small patties. Dust with flour and put on a non-stick baking sheet, then grill for 3 minutes on each side. Serve the fishcakes hot, with watercress.

Serves 4	EASY		NUTRITIONAL INFORMATION	
	Preparation Time 15 minutes	**Cooking Time** 25 minutes	**Per Serving** 196 calories, 5g fat (of which 1g saturates), 27g carbohydrate, 0.1g salt	Gluten free Dairy free

Scallops with Sweet and Sour Cucumber

18 large fresh scallops, without roe, well chilled

juice of 2 limes

2 tbsp golden caster sugar

1 tbsp white wine vinegar

½ cucumber, seeded and diced

2 tbsp mild extra virgin olive oil

pickled ginger

salt and ground black pepper

a bunch of watercress, well washed, to garnish

1 Trim and discard any hard muscle from the side of the scallops, then slice each one very thinly crossways. Arrange in a single layer on a large plate and squeeze the juice of 1½ limes over the top. Cover and chill for 2 hours.

2 Put the sugar, a pinch of salt, plenty of pepper and 2 tbsp boiling water into a bowl, then stir to dissolve the sugar. Mix in the vinegar, add the cucumber, cover the bowl and chill for 1 hour.

3 Pour the remaining lime juice into a small bowl, add a pinch of salt and a little pepper and whisk. Whisk in the oil to make a dressing.

4 Remove the scallops from the lime juice and arrange the slices in pairs on individual plates. Using a slotted spoon, put some drained cucumber in the centre and top with slivers of pickled ginger. Drizzle the dressing over the scallops and arrange watercress sprigs around them.

EASY	NUTRITIONAL INFORMATION		Serves
Preparation Time 20 minutes, plus chilling time	**Per Serving** 133 calories, 5g fat (of which 1g saturates), 8g carbohydrate, 0.3g salt	Gluten free Dairy free	**6**

Roasted Cod with Fennel

50g (2oz) butter

1 tbsp olive oil

2 red onions, finely sliced

2 small or 1 large fennel bulb, trimmed and finely sliced

2 tbsp chopped dill, plus extra to garnish

150ml (¼ pint) dry white wine

4 x 150g (5oz) pieces cod

salt and ground black pepper

new potatoes and green beans to serve

1 Preheat the oven to 200°C (180°C fan oven) mark 6. Heat the butter and oil in a flameproof casserole dish over a medium heat. When sizzling, add the onions and fennel, then cover and cook, stirring occasionally, for 7 minutes or until soft and translucent.

2 Add the dill and wine and bring quickly to the boil. Put the fish on top of the fennel mixture and season with salt and pepper. Put the casserole dish in the oven and cook for 10 minutes, basting the fish occasionally with the juices.

3 Sprinkle with plenty of extra dill and serve immediately with new potatoes and green beans.

Try Something Different

Use haddock, coley or whiting instead of the cod.
Stir 1 tbsp capers in with the dill and wine.

EASY		NUTRITIONAL INFORMATION		Serves
Preparation Time 3 minutes	**Cooking Time** 20 minutes	**Per Serving** 306 calories, 14g fat (of which 7g saturates), 9g carbohydrate, 0.4g salt	Gluten free Dairy free	**4**

Try Something Different

Use another fish instead of salmon; try trout or plump mackerel fillets.

Salmon with a Spicy Yogurt Crust

3 tbsp freshly chopped coriander

1 garlic clove, crushed

2.5cm (1in) piece fresh root ginger, peeled and grated

½ tsp each ground cumin and coriander

¼ tsp cayenne pepper

150g (5oz) natural yogurt

4 x 125g (4oz) salmon fillets

salt

lime wedges and herb salad to serve

1   Preheat the grill. Mix together the chopped coriander, garlic, ginger, cumin, ground coriander, cayenne, yogurt and a pinch of salt. Add the salmon and turn to coat.

2   Grill the fish for 7–10 minutes or until cooked through. Serve with lime wedges to squeeze over the fish and a herb salad.

Serves	EASY		NUTRITIONAL INFORMATION	
4	**Preparation Time** 10 minutes	**Cooking Time** 10 minutes	**Per Serving** 250 calories, 14g fat (of which 3g saturates), 3g carbohydrate, 0.2g salt	Gluten free

Try Something Different

Instead of pork, use the same quantity of lean lamb, such as leg, trimmed of excess fat and cut into cubes.

Warming Winter Casserole

2 tbsp olive oil

500g (1lb 2oz) pork fillet, cubed

1 onion, finely chopped

2 garlic cloves, finely chopped

1 tsp ground cinnamon

1 tbsp ground coriander

1 tsp ground cumin

2.5cm (1in) piece fresh root ginger, peeled and grated

400g can mixed beans or chickpeas, drained

1 red pepper, seeded and sliced

50g (2oz) ready-to-eat dried apricots, roughly chopped

300ml (½ pint) chicken stock

25g (1oz) flaked almonds, toasted

salt and ground black pepper

freshly chopped flat-leafed parsley to garnish

brown basmati rice to serve

1 Heat 1 tbsp oil in a flameproof casserole, add the pork and fry, in batches, until brown all over. Remove and set aside. Add the remaining oil, then add the onion and cook for 10 minutes until softened. Return the pork to the casserole, add the garlic, spices and ginger and cook for 2 minutes.

2 Add the mixed beans, red pepper, apricots and stock. Season well with salt and pepper, then stir and bring to the boil. Reduce the heat to the lowest setting and simmer, covered, for 40 minutes, adding a little extra stock if it begins to looks dry.

3 Sprinkle with the almonds and parsley, check the seasoning and serve with brown basmati rice.

EASY		NUTRITIONAL INFORMATION		Serves
Preparation Time 20 minutes	**Cooking Time** 1 hour	**Per Serving** 407 calories; 16g fat (of which 3g saturates), 32g carbohydrate, 1g salt	Gluten free Dairy free	**4**

Cook's Tip

Colcannon: cook 1.1kg (2½lb) floury potatoes in salted boiling water until tender. Drain in a colander. Add 25g (1oz) butter to the pan and gently fry 1 chopped leek or 100g (3½oz) shredded cabbage until soft. Return the potato to the pan with another 25g (1oz) butter and a handful of chopped herbs such as parsley, chives and thyme. Heat through gently.

Sausages with Red Onion Marmalade

12 gluten-free (100% meat) venison sausages

6 tsp redcurrant jelly

For the red onion marmalade

400g (14oz) red onions, chopped

2 tbsp olive oil

4 tbsp red wine vinegar

2 tbsp demerara sugar

1 tsp juniper berries, crushed

colcannon (see Cook's Tip) or mashed potatoes to serve

1 Preheat the oven to 220°C (200°C fan oven) mark 7. Put the sausages into a small roasting tin. Roast in the oven for 35 minutes, turning once.

2 After 25 minutes, spoon the redcurrant jelly over and continue to cook.

3 Meanwhile, make the red onion marmalade. Gently fry the red onions in the olive oil for 15–20 minutes. Add the vinegar, sugar and juniper berries, and cook for a further 5 minutes until the onions are very tender. Serve the sausages with the red onion marmalade and colcannon.

Serves	EASY		NUTRITIONAL INFORMATION	
6	**Preparation Time** 15 minutes	**Cooking Time** 35 minutes	**Per Serving** 390 calories, 25g fat (of which 10g saturates), 14g carbohydrate, 0.3g salt	Gluten free Dairy free

Try Something Different

Use chicken pieces such as drumsticks or thighs, reducing the cooking time in step 4 to 20 minutes.

2 tbsp olive oil

1 large onion, cut into wedges

2 rindless streaky bacon rashers, chopped

1.6kg (3½lb) organic or free-range chicken

6 carrots

2 small turnips, cut into wedges

1 garlic clove, crushed

bouquet garni (1 bay leaf, few parsley and thyme sprigs)

600ml (1 pint) hot chicken stock

100ml (3½fl oz) dry white wine

12 button mushrooms

3 tbsp freshly chopped flat-leafed parsley

salt and ground black pepper

mashed potatoes to serve

One-pot Chicken

1 Heat the oil in a non-stick flameproof casserole dish, then add the onion and bacon and fry for 5 minutes until golden. Remove and set aside.

2 Add the whole chicken to the casserole and fry for 10 minutes, turning carefully to brown all over. Remove and set aside.

3 Preheat the oven to 200°C (180°C fan oven) mark 6. Add the carrots, turnips and garlic to the casserole. Fry for 5 minutes, return the bacon and onion, and put the chicken back in. Add the bouquet garni, stock and wine. Season with salt and pepper. Bring to a simmer, then cover and cook in the oven for 30 minutes.

4 Remove the casserole from the oven and add the mushrooms. Baste the chicken, then re-cover and cook for a further 50 minutes.

5 Stir in the parsley. Lift out the chicken, carve and serve with the vegetables, cooking liquid and mashed potatoes.

EASY		NUTRITIONAL INFORMATION		Serves
Preparation Time 20 minutes	**Cooking Time** 1 hour 40 minutes	**Per Serving** 474 calories, 33g fat (of which 9g saturates), 6g carbohydrate, 0.6g salt	Gluten free Dairy free	**6**

Oriental Beef Salad

4 tbsp tamari (wheat-free Japanese soy sauce), plus extra to serve

juice of ½ lime

2 x 175g (6oz) sirloin steaks

1 tbsp vegetable oil

1 mango, peeled, stoned and sliced

4 spring onions, sliced

½ Chinese lettuce, finely sliced

150g (5oz) bean sprouts

1 tbsp sesame seeds, toasted

2 tbsp freshly chopped coriander

lime wedges to serve

1 In a bowl, mix together the tamari and lime juice. Spoon half the dressing over the steaks and set the remainder aside.

2 Heat the oil in a frying pan, add the steaks and fry for 2 minutes on each side for medium rare, or 3–4 minutes for well done. Set aside.

3 Put the mango, spring onions, lettuce and bean sprouts into a large bowl. Add the remaining dressing and toss gently. Slice the steak into 1cm (½in) strips and serve with the salad. Sprinkle with sesame seeds and coriander and serve with a wedge of lime. Serve extra tamari sauce in a small bowl.

Try Something Different

For an alternative dressing, mix together 2 tbsp tamari, 1 tbsp clear honey and 1 tbsp mirin (sweet Japanese rice wine).

Serves 4	EASY		NUTRITIONAL INFORMATION	
	Preparation Time 10 minutes	**Cooking Time** 10 minutes	**Per Serving** 214 calories, 9g fat (of which 3g saturates), 9g carbohydrate, 2.8g salt	Gluten free Dairy free

700g (1½lb) braising steak, cut into large chunks about 5cm (2in) across

2 tsp plain gluten-free flour

2 tbsp oil

25g (1oz) butter

2 large onions, finely sliced

225g (8oz) carrots, cut into large sticks

200ml (7fl oz) Guinness

300ml (½ pint) vegetable stock

2 tsp tomato purée

2 tsp English mustard

2 tsp light muscovado sugar

225g (8oz) large field mushrooms

salt and ground black pepper

mashed potatoes and rocket leaves to serve

Beef with Beer and Mushrooms

1 Preheat the oven to 150°C (130°C fan oven) mark 2. Toss the meat in the flour. Heat the oil and butter in a large casserole dish over a medium heat and brown the meat, a few pieces at a time, removing it with a slotted spoon. The flavour and colour of the finished casserole depend on the meat taking on a good deep colour now. Stir the onions into the casserole and cook for about 10 minutes.

2 Return all the meat to the casserole, add the carrots, then stir in the Guinness, stock, tomato purée, mustard, sugar and plenty of seasoning. Bring to the boil, stir well, then cover tightly with foil or a lid and simmer gently in the oven for 1½ hours.

3 Stir the whole mushrooms into the casserole and return to the oven for a further 45 minutes–1 hour until the meat is meltingly tender. Serve with mashed potatoes and rocket leaves.

Serves 4	EASY		NUTRITIONAL INFORMATION	
	Preparation Time 15 minutes	**Cooking Time** 2¾–3 hours	**Per Serving** 450 calories, 22g fat (of which 8g saturates), 21g carbohydrate, 0.6g salt	Gluten free Dairy free

▶ *Start the day:* Apple Compote
(see page 34)
▶ *Lunch:* Roasted Tomato and Pepper Soup
(see page 45)
▼ Curried Lamb with Lentils

Curried Lamb with Lentils

500g (1lb 2oz) lean stewing lamb on
the bone, cut into 8 pieces (ask your butcher
to do this), trimmed of fat

1 tsp ground cumin

1 tsp ground turmeric

2 garlic cloves, crushed

1 medium red chilli, seeded and chopped
(see page 49)

2.5cm (1in) piece fresh root ginger, peeled and grated

2 tbsp rapeseed oil

1 onion, chopped

400g can chopped tomatoes

2 tbsp vinegar

175g (6oz) red lentils, rinsed

salt and ground black pepper

coriander sprigs to garnish

rocket salad to serve

1 Put the lamb into a shallow sealable container,
add the spices, garlic, chilli, ginger, salt and pepper.
Stir well to mix, then cover and chill for at least
30 minutes.

2 Heat the oil in a large flameproof casserole dish, add
the onion and cook over a low heat for 5 minutes.
Add the lamb and cook for 10 minutes, turning
regularly, until the meat is evenly browned.

3 Add the chopped tomatoes, vinegar, 450ml (¾ pint)
boiling water and the lentils, and bring to the boil.
Reduce the heat, cover and simmer for 1 hour.
Remove the lid and cook for 30 minutes, stirring
occasionally, until the sauce is thick and the lamb is
tender. Serve hot, garnished with coriander, with a
rocket salad.

EASY		**NUTRITIONAL INFORMATION**		Serves
Preparation Time 15 minutes, plus marinating	**Cooking Time** 1 hour 50 minutes	**Per Serving** 433 calories, 16g fat (of which 7g saturates), 38g carbohydrate, 0.3g salt	Gluten free Dairy free	**4**

Braised Lamb Shanks with Cannellini Beans

3 tbsp olive oil

6 lamb shanks

1 large onion, chopped

3 carrots, sliced

3 celery sticks, sliced

2 garlic cloves, crushed

2 x 400g cans chopped tomatoes

125ml (4fl oz) balsamic vinegar

2 bay leaves

2 x 400g cans cannellini beans, drained and rinsed

salt and ground black pepper

steamed spinach to serve

1 Preheat the oven to 170°C (150°C fan oven) mark 3. Heat the oil in a large flameproof casserole dish and brown the lamb shanks, in two batches, all over. Remove and set aside.

2 Add the onion, carrots, celery and garlic to the casserole dish and cook gently until softened and just beginning to colour.

3 Return the lamb to the casserole and add the chopped tomatoes and balsamic vinegar, giving the mixture a good stir. Season with salt and pepper and add the bay leaves. Bring to a simmer, cover and cook on the hob for 5 minutes.

4 Transfer to the oven and cook for 1½–2 hours or until the lamb shanks are nearly tender.

5 Remove the casserole from the oven and add the cannellini beans. Cover and return to the oven for a further 30 minutes. Serve with spinach.

EASY		NUTRITIONAL INFORMATION		Serves
Preparation Time 15 minutes	**Cooking Time** 3 hours	**Per Serving** 382 calories, 18g fat (of which 6g saturates), 29g carbohydrate, 1.2g salt	Gluten free Dairy free	**6**

Vegetable Moussaka

450g (1lb) potatoes, cut lengthways into 5mm (¼in) slices

1 aubergine, sliced into rounds

1 large red onion, cut into wedges

2 red peppers, seeded and sliced

4 tbsp olive oil

2 tbsp chopped thyme

225g (8oz) tomatoes, thickly sliced

2 garlic cloves, sliced

250g (9oz) passata

250g (9oz) soft goat's cheese

300g (11oz) natural yogurt

3 medium eggs

25g (1oz) freshly grated Parmesan

salt and ground black pepper

1 Preheat the oven to 230°C (210°C fan oven) mark 8. Boil the potatoes in a pan of salted water for 5 minutes. Drain and put into a large roasting tin with the aubergine, onion and peppers. Drizzle with oil, add the thyme, toss and season with salt and pepper. Roast for 30 minutes, stirring occasionally.

2 Add the tomatoes and garlic and roast for 15 minutes, then take out of the oven. Reduce the oven temperature to 200°C (180°C fan oven) mark 6.

3 Put half the vegetables in a 1.7 litre (3 pint) ovenproof dish, then spoon half the passata over them and spread the goat's cheese on top. Repeat with the rest of the vegetables and passata. Mix together the yogurt, eggs and Parmesan. Season and then pour over the top. Cook in the oven for 45 minutes or until heated through.

Try Something Different

Use sliced sweet potatoes, or butternut squash, seeded and cut into chunks, instead of the potatoes.

Serves	EASY		NUTRITIONAL INFORMATION	
6	Preparation Time 45 minutes	Cooking Time 1½ hours	Per Serving 399 calories, 24g fat (of which 11g saturates), 29g carbohydrate, 1.2g salt	Gluten free

Try Something Different

Instead of the squash use 750g (1lb 10oz) peeled and seeded pumpkin.
Instead of the onion use a fennel bulb.

Squash and Pancetta Risotto

125g (4oz) pancetta or smoked bacon, chopped

1 small butternut squash, peeled and cut into small chunks

1 onion, finely chopped

300g (11oz) arborio (risotto) rice

1 litre (1¾ pints) hot vegetable stock

1 Put the pancetta or bacon and the butternut squash into a large, deep frying pan and fry over a medium heat for 8–10 minutes.

2 When the pancetta is golden and the squash has softened, add the onion to the pan and continue to fry for 5 minutes until softened.

3 Stir in the rice, cook for 1–2 minutes, then add the stock. Bring to the boil and simmer for 15–20 minutes, stirring occasionally to ensure that the rice doesn't stick, until almost all the stock has been absorbed and the rice and squash are tender. Serve immediately.

Serves 4	EASY		NUTRITIONAL INFORMATION	
	Preparation Time 10 minutes	**Cooking Time** 40 minutes	**Per Serving** 390 calories, 9g fat (of which 3g saturates), 65g carbohydrate, 2g salt	Gluten free Dairy free

Polenta with Mixed Mushrooms

50g (2oz) butter

1.1kg (2½lb) mixed mushrooms

1 red chilli, seeded and finely chopped (see page 49)

3 garlic cloves, sliced

100g (3½oz) sun-dried tomatoes, roughly chopped

1 tsp chopped thyme, plus thyme sprigs to garnish

1kg (2¼lb) ready-made polenta

3 tbsp olive oil

truffle oil (optional)

salt and ground black pepper

1 Melt half the butter in a deep-sided frying pan or wok. Add half the mushrooms and cook over a high heat until all the liquid has evaporated, then set aside. Repeat with the remaining butter and mushrooms. Add the chilli and garlic to the pan and fry for 2 minutes, then add to the mushrooms, together with the sun-dried tomatoes and thyme. Mix well and season with salt and pepper.

2 Slice the polenta into 12 pieces, about 1cm (½in) thick. Heat the olive oil in a non-stick frying pan. Add the polenta in batches, and fry for 3–4 minutes on each side or until golden.

3 To serve, arrange two slices of polenta per person on a plate, top with the mushroom mixture and drizzle with a little truffle oil, if using. Garnish with thyme sprigs.

EASY		NUTRITIONAL INFORMATION		Serves
Preparation Time 10 minutes	**Cooking Time** 20 minutes	**Per Serving** 383 calories, 13g fat (of which 4g saturates), 56g carbohydrate, 0.1g salt	Vegetarian Gluten free	**6**

5

Treats

Health Tip

This is the perfect dessert after a heavy or rich meal. Fresh pineapple contains an enzyme, bromelin, which digests protein very effectively and helps balance any excess acidity or alkalinity. Ginger is a well-known digestive and has many therapeutic properties.

Ginger-glazed Pineapple

2 pineapples
2 tbsp light muscovado sugar
2 tsp ground ginger
natural yogurt and honey to serve

1   Cut the pineapples into quarters lengthways, leaving the stalk intact. Remove the core, extract the flesh, and reserve the skin. Cut the flesh into pieces and return to the pineapple shell. Wrap the green leaves of the stalk in foil.

2   Preheat the grill. Mix together the sugar and ginger. Sprinkle each pineapple quarter with the sugar mixture. Put on foil-lined baking sheets and grill for 10 minutes until golden and caramelised. Serve with natural yogurt and a drizzle of runny honey.

Serves 6	EASY		NUTRITIONAL INFORMATION	
	Preparation Time 10 minutes	**Cooking Time** 10 minutes	**Per Serving** 88 calories, trace fat, 22g carbohydrate, 0g salt	Vegetarian Gluten free • Dairy free

Try Something Different

Use blackberries instead of rhubarb: you will need 400g (14oz), and a squeeze of lemon juice instead of the orange juice. Blend in a food processor after stirring in the redcurrant jelly.

Rhubarb Fool

450g (1lb) rhubarb, thickly chopped

50ml (2fl oz) orange juice

1 cinnamon stick

25g (1oz) golden caster sugar

1 tbsp redcurrant jelly

150g (5oz) fat-free Greek-style yogurt

2 tbsp soft brown sugar

1   Put the rhubarb, orange juice, cinnamon stick and caster sugar into a pan. Cover and cook gently for 10 minutes or until tender.

2   Remove the lid and cook for 5 minutes until the liquid has evaporated. Discard the cinnamon stick. Stir in the redcurrant jelly then leave to cool.

3   Roughly fold in the yogurt, then spoon the mixture into six glasses and sprinkle with the soft brown sugar. Chill for 2 hours.

EASY		NUTRITIONAL INFORMATION		Serves
Preparation Time 5 minutes, plus chilling	**Cooking Time** 10 minutes	**Per Serving** 107 calories, 3g fat (of which 1g saturates), 20g carbohydrate, 0.1g salt	Vegetarian Gluten free	**6**

Apple and Raspberry Mousse

900g (2lb) cooking apples, peeled, cored and sliced
4 tbsp orange juice
grated zest of 1 lemon
225g (8oz) raspberries
6 tbsp golden caster sugar
1 large egg white
mint sprigs to decorate

1 Put the apples and orange juice into a pan and cook over a low heat, uncovered, for 10 minutes until soft. Add the lemon zest, then use a fork to mash to a purée. Cover and chill for at least 1 hour.

2 Gently heat the raspberries and 2 tbsp sugar in a pan until the juices start to run.

3 Whisk the egg white in a clean grease-free bowl until stiff, adding the remaining sugar gradually until the mixture forms stiff peaks. Fold into the apple purée.

4 Divide the raspberries and any juice among six serving glasses, spoon the apple mixture on top and decorate with mint sprigs.

EASY		NUTRITIONAL INFORMATION		Serves
Preparation Time 10 minutes, plus chilling	**Cooking Time** 15 minutes	**Per Serving** 127 calories, trace fat, 32g carbohydrate, 0g salt	Vegetarian Gluten free • Dairy free	**6**

Try Something Different

Use nectarines instead of peaches, or 8 plump plums.

Griddled Peaches

4 ripe but firm peaches

1 tbsp maple syrup

1 tsp light olive oil

25g (1oz) pecan nuts, toasted

1 Halve the peaches and carefully remove the stones. Cut the flesh into thick slices, then put into a bowl with the maple syrup and toss to coat.

2 Heat the oil in a griddle or large frying pan, add the peaches and cook for 3–4 minutes on each side until starting to char and caramelise. Sprinkle with the toasted pecan nuts and serve at once.

Serves 4	EASY		NUTRITIONAL INFORMATION	
	Preparation Time 15 minutes	**Cooking Time** 6–8 minutes	**Per Serving** 94 calories, 5g fat (of which 1g saturates), 11g carbohydrate, 0g salt	Vegetarian Gluten free • Dairy free

Try Something Different

Use 2 papayas, peeled, seeded and chopped, instead of the pineapple. Mix the seeds of 2 passion fruit with the lime juice before adding to the salad.

Exotic Fruit Salad

2 oranges
1 mango, peeled, stoned and chopped
450g (1lb) peeled and diced fresh pineapple
200g (7oz) blueberries
$\frac{1}{2}$ Charentais melon, cubed
grated zest and juice of 1 lime

1 Using a sharp knife, peel the oranges, remove the pith and cut into segments. Put into a bowl.

2 Add the mango to the bowl with the pineapple, blueberries and melon.

3 Add the lime zest and juice, and gently mix together. Serve immediately.

EASY	NUTRITIONAL INFORMATION		Serves
Preparation Time: 10 minutes	**Per Serving:** 187 calories, 1g fat, 47g carbohydrate, 0.1g salt	Vegetarian Gluten free • Dairy free	**4**

Strawberries with Chocolate Meringue

225g (8oz) strawberries, chopped
finely grated zest of ½ orange
125g (4oz) caster sugar, plus 1 tbsp extra
3 large egg whites
1 tbsp cocoa powder, sifted
15g (½oz) hazelnuts, toasted and chopped

1 Preheat the oven to 150°C (130°C fan oven) mark 2. Mix together the strawberries, orange zest and 1 tbsp caster sugar. Divide among six ramekins.

2 Put the egg whites into a clean grease-free bowl and whisk until soft peaks form. Add the remaining sugar and whisk until the whites are stiff and shiny. Fold in the cocoa.

3 Spoon the chocolate meringue over the fruit and sprinkle the hazelnuts on top.

4 Bake in the oven for 20–25 minutes until the meringue is crisp on the outside and soft in the middle. Serve immediately.

Try Something Different

Use raspberries instead of strawberries, leaving them whole.
Try lightly toasted flaked almonds instead of the hazelnuts.

Serves 6	EASY		NUTRITIONAL INFORMATION	
	Preparation Time 15 minutes	**Cooking Time** 20–25 minutes	**Per Serving** 132 calories, 2g fat (of which trace saturates), 27g carbohydrate, 0.1g salt	Vegetarian Gluten free • Dairy free

Chocolate Cherry Roll

4 tbsp cocoa powder, plus extra to dust

100ml (3$\frac{1}{2}$fl oz) milk, plus 3 tbsp extra

5 medium eggs, separated

125g (4oz) golden caster sugar

1–2 tbsp cherry jam

400g can cherries without stones, drained and chopped

icing sugar to dust

1 Preheat the oven to 180°C (160°C fan oven) mark 4. Line a 30 x 20cm (12 x 8in) Swiss roll tin with baking parchment. In a bowl, mix together the cocoa and 3 tbsp milk. Heat 100ml (3$\frac{1}{2}$fl oz) milk in a pan until almost boiling, then add to the bowl, stirring. Leave to cool for 10 minutes.

2 Whisk the egg whites in a clean grease-free bowl until soft peaks form. In a separate bowl, whisk together the egg yolks and caster sugar until pale and thick. Gradually whisk in the cooled milk, then fold in the egg whites. Spoon the mixture into the prepared tin and smooth the surface. Bake in the oven for 25 minutes or until just firm.

3 Turn out on to a board lined with baking parchment and peel off the lining parchment. Cover with a damp tea towel.

4 Spread the jam over the sponge and top with the cherries. Roll up from the shortest end, dust with cocoa and icing sugar, then cut into slices and serve.

Try Something Different

You can add whipped cream to the roulade, but you will need to cool it first. To do this, turn out the roulade on to baking parchment. Do not remove the lining paper but roll the roulade around it while still warm. Leave to cool, unroll and peel off the paper. Spread with the jam and fruit, then the cream, and re-roll.

A LITTLE EFFORT		NUTRITIONAL INFORMATION		Serves
Preparation Time 30 minutes	**Cooking Time** 30 minutes, plus cooling	**Per Serving** 185 calories, 5g fat (of which 2g saturates), 30g carbohydrate, 0.3g salt	Vegetarian Gluten free	**8**

Luxury Chocolate Orange Torte

75g (3oz) butter, diced, plus extra to grease

100g (3½oz) plain chocolate (at least 70% cocoa solids), broken into pieces

6 medium eggs

225g (8oz) golden caster sugar

150g (5oz) ground almonds, sifted

grated zest and juice of 1 orange

strawberries and raspberries to serve

1 Preheat the oven to 190°C (170°C fan oven) mark 5. Grease a 20cm (8in) springform cake tin and line with greaseproof paper.

2 Melt the butter and chocolate in a bowl set over a pan of gently simmering water. Remove the bowl from the pan and set aside to cool a little.

3 Put the eggs and sugar into a large bowl and mix with an electric whisk until the volume has tripled and the mixture is thick and foamy – it will take about 5–10 minutes. Add the ground almonds, orange zest and juice to the egg mixture, then gently fold together with a metal spoon.

4 Pour about two-thirds of the mixture into the prepared tin. Add the melted chocolate and butter to the remaining mixture and fold together. Add to the tin and swirl around just once or twice to create a marbled effect. Bake in the oven for 50 minutes–1 hour. Leave to cool in the tin, then carefully remove and slice. Serve with strawberries and raspberries.

Serves 12	A LITTLE EFFORT		NUTRITIONAL INFORMATION	
	Preparation Time 30 minutes	**Cooking Time** 55 minutes – 1 hour 5 minutes	**Per Serving** 231 calories, 12g fat (of which 3g saturates), 25g carbohydrate, 0.1g salt	Vegetarian Gluten free

Cook's Tip

Wrap in clingfilm and store in an airtight container. It will keep for up to five days.

Fruity Teacake

150ml (¼ pint) hot black tea, made with 2 Earl Grey teabags

200g (7oz) sultanas

75g (3oz) ready-to-eat dried figs, roughly chopped

75g (3oz) ready-to-eat prunes, roughly chopped

a little vegetable oil

125g (4oz) dark muscovado sugar

2 medium eggs, beaten

225g (8oz) gluten-free flour

2 tsp wheat-free baking powder

2 tsp ground mixed spice

1 Pour the tea into a bowl and add all the dried fruit. Leave to soak for 30 minutes.

2 Preheat the oven to 190°C (170°C fan oven) mark 5. Oil a 900g (2lb) loaf tin and line the base with greaseproof paper.

3 In a large bowl, beat together the muscovado sugar and eggs until pale and slightly thickened. Add the flour, baking powder, ground mixed spice and soaked dried fruit and tea, then mix together well.

4 Spoon the mixture into the prepared tin and bake in the centre of the oven for 45 minutes–1 hour. Leave to cool.

5 Serve sliced, with a little butter if you like.

EASY		NUTRITIONAL INFORMATION		Serves
Preparation Time 20 minutes, plus soaking	**Cooking Time** 1 hour	**Per Serving** 185 calories, 1g fat (of which trace saturates), 42g carbohydrate, 0.1g salt	Vegetarian Gluten free • Dairy free	**12**

Sticky Lemon Polenta Cake

50g (2oz) softened butter, plus extra for greasing

3 lemons

250g (9oz) golden caster sugar

250g (9oz) instant polenta

1 tsp wheat-free baking powder

2 large eggs

50ml (2fl oz) semi-skimmed milk

2 tbsp natural yogurt

2 tbsp poppy seeds

1 Preheat the oven to 180°C (160°C fan oven) mark 4. Lightly grease a 900g (2lb) loaf tin and line the base with greaseproof paper .

2 Grate the zest of 1 lemon and put into a food processor with the butter, 200g (7oz) sugar, the polenta, baking powder, eggs, milk, yogurt and poppy seeds and whiz until smooth. Spoon the mixture into the prepared tin and smooth the top. Bake in the oven for 55 minutes–1 hour or until a skewer inserted into the centre comes out clean. Leave to cool in the tin for 10 minutes.

3 Next, make a syrup. Squeeze the juice from the zested lemon plus 1 more lemon. Thinly slice the third lemon. Put into a pan with the remaining sugar and 150ml (¼ pint) water. Bring to the boil and bubble for about 10 minutes until syrupy, then remove from the heat.

4 Slide a knife around the edge of the cake and turn out on to a serving plate. Pierce the cake in several places with a skewer, spoon the syrup over it and decorate with lemon slices.

Cook's Tip

Wrap in clingfilm and store in an airtight container for up to three days.

A LITTLE EFFORT		NUTRITIONAL INFORMATION		Serves
Preparation Time 10 minutes	**Cooking Time** 1 hour, plus cooling	**Per Serving** 220 calories, 7g fat (of which 3g saturates), 37g carbohydrate, 0.1g salt	Vegetarian Gluten free	**12**

Spiced Star Biscuits

2 tbsp runny honey

25g (1oz) unsalted butter

50g (2oz) light muscovado sugar

finely grated zest of ½ lemon

finely grated zest of ½ orange

225g (8oz) gluten-free flour, plus extra to dust

1 tsp wheat-free baking powder

1 tsp ground cinnamon

1 tsp ground ginger

½ tsp freshly grated nutmeg

pinch of ground cloves

pinch of salt

1 tbsp finely chopped candied peel

50g (2oz) ground almonds

1 large egg, beaten

2–3 tbsp milk

icing and silver balls to decorate (optional)

1. Put the honey, butter, sugar and citrus zests into a small pan and stir over a low heat until the butter has melted and the ingredients are well combined.

2. Sift the flour, baking powder, spices and salt together in a bowl, then add the chopped candied peel and ground almonds. Add the melted mixture, beaten egg and milk, and mix until the dough comes together, adding a little extra milk if the dough feels crumbly. Knead the dough briefly until smooth, then wrap in clingfilm and chill for at least 4 hours or overnight.

3. Preheat the oven to 180°C (160°C fan oven) mark 4. Roll out the dough on a lightly floured surface to a thickness of 5mm (¼in). Stamp out stars, using a 5cm (2in) cutter, and put on several baking sheets.

4. Bake in the oven for 15–20 minutes until just beginning to brown at the edges. Transfer the biscuits to a wire rack to cool. Store in an airtight tin for up to a week. If you like, decorate some of the biscuits with icing and silver balls.

Makes 35	EASY		NUTRITIONAL INFORMATION	
	Preparation Time 15 minutes, plus chilling	**Cooking Time** 15–20 minutes, plus cooling	**Per Biscuit** 51 calories, 2g fat (of which 1g saturates), 8g carbohydrate, 0g salt	Vegetarian Gluten free

Glossary

Al dente Italian term commonly used to describe food, especially pasta and vegetables, which are cooked until tender but still firm to the bite.

Baking blind Pre-baking a pastry case before filling. The pastry case is lined with greaseproof paper and weighted down with dried beans or ceramic baking beans.

Baste To spoon the juices and melted fat over meat, poultry, game or vegetables during roasting to keep them moist. The term is also used to describe spooning over a marinade.

Beat To incorporate air into an ingredient or mixture by agitating it vigorously with a spoon, fork, whisk or electric mixer. The technique is also used to soften ingredients.

Bind To mix beaten egg or other liquid into a dry mixture to hold it together.

Blanch To immerse food briefly in fast-boiling water to loosen skins, such as peaches or tomatoes, or to remove bitterness, or to destroy enzymes and preserve the colour, flavour and texture of vegetables (especially prior to freezing).

Bouquet garni Small bunch of herbs – usually a mixture of parsley stems, thyme and a bay leaf – tied in muslin and used to flavour stocks, soups and stews.

Braise To cook meat, poultry, game or vegetables slowly in a small amount of liquid in a pan or casserole with a tight-fitting lid. The food is usually first browned in oil or fat.

Caramelise To heat sugar or sugar syrup slowly until it is brown in colour; ie forms a caramel.

Chill To cool food in the fridge.

Compote Fresh or dried fruit stewed in sugar syrup. Served hot or cold.

Coulis A smooth fruit or vegetable purée, thinned if necessary to a pouring consistency.

Cream To beat together fat and sugar until the mixture is pale and fluffy, and resembles whipped cream in texture and colour. The method is used in cakes and puddings which contain a high proportion of fat and require the incorporation of a lot of air.

Croûtons Small pieces of fried or toasted bread, served with soups and salads.

Crudités Raw vegetables, usually cut into slices or sticks, typically served with a dipping sauce.

Curdle To cause sauces or creamed mixtures to separate, usually by overheating or over-beating.

Cure To preserve fish, meat or poultry by smoking, drying or salting.

Deglaze To heat stock, wine or other liquid with the cooking juices left in the pan after roasting or sautéeing, scraping and stirring vigorously to dissolve the sediment on the bottom of the pan.

Dice To cut food into small cubes.

Dredge To sprinkle food generously with flour, sugar, icing sugar etc.

Dust To sprinkle lightly with flour, cornflour, icing sugar etc.

Escalope Thin slice of meat, such as pork, veal or turkey, from the top of the leg, usually pan-fried.

Fillet Term used to describe boned breasts of birds, boned sides of fish, and the undercut of a loin of beef, lamb, pork or veal.

Flake To separate food, such as cooked fish, into natural pieces.

Folding in Method of combining a whisked or creamed mixture with other ingredients by cutting and folding so that it retains its lightness. A large metal spoon or plastic-bladed spatula is used.

Fry To cook food in hot fat or oil. There are various methods: shallow-frying in a little fat in a shallow pan; deep-frying where the food is totally immersed in oil; dry-frying in which fatty foods are cooked in a non-stick pan without extra fat; see also Stir-frying.

Garnish A decoration, usually edible, such as parsley or lemon, which is used to enhance the appearance of a savoury dish.

Gluten A protein constituent of grains, such as wheat and rye, which develops when the flour is missed with water to give the dough elasticity.

Griddle A flat, heavy, metal plate used on the hob for cooking scones or for searing savoury ingredients.

Gut To clean out the entrails from fish.

Hull To remove the stalk and calyx from soft fruits, such as strawberries.

Infuse To immerse flavourings, such as aromatic vegetables, herbs, spices and vanilla, in a liquid to impart flavour. Usually the infused liquid is brought to the boil, then left to stand for a while.

Julienne Fine 'matchstick' strips of vegetables or citrus zest, sometimes used as a garnish.

Macerate To soften and flavour raw or dried foods by soaking in a liquid, eg soaking fruit in alcohol.

Marinate To soak raw meat, poultry or game – usually in a mixture of oil, wine, vinegar and flavourings – to soften and impart flavour. The mixture, which is known as a marinade, may also be used to baste the food during cooking.

Medallion Small round piece of meat, usually beef or veal.

Mince To cut food into very fine pieces, using a mincer, food processor or knife.

Parboil To boil a vegetable or other food for part of its cooking time before finishing it by another method.

Pare To finely peel the skin or zest from vegetables or fruit.

Poach To cook food gently in liquid at simmering point; the surface should be just trembling.

Pot roast To cook meat in a covered pan with some fat and a little liquid.

Purée To pound, sieve or liquidise vegetables, fish or fruit to a smooth pulp. Purées often form the basis for soups and sauces.

Reduce To fast-boil stock or other liquid in an uncovered pan to evaporate water and concentrate the flavour.

Refresh To cool hot vegetables very quickly by plunging into ice-cold water or holding under cold running water in order to stop the cooking process and preserve the colour.

Roast To cook food by dry heat in the oven.

Roux A mixture of equal quantities of butter (or other fat) and flour cooked together to form the basis of many sauces.

Rubbing in Method of incorporating fat into flour by rubbing between the fingertips, used when a short texture is required. Used for pastry, cakes, scones and biscuits.

Salsa Piquant sauce made from chopped fresh vegetables and sometimes fruit.

Sauté To cook food in a small quantity of fat over a high heat, shaking the pan constantly – usually in a sauté pan (a frying pan with straight sides and a wide base).

Scald To pour boiling water over food to clean it, or loosen skin, eg tomatoes. Also used to describe heating milk to just below boiling point.

Score To cut parallel lines in the surface of food, such as fish (or the fat layer on meat), to improve its appearance or help it cook more quickly.

Sear To brown meat quickly in a little hot fat before grilling or roasting.

Seasoned flour Flour mixed with a little salt and pepper, used for dusting meat, fish etc., before frying.

Shred To grate cheese or slice vegetables into very fine pieces or strips.

Sieve To press food through a perforated sieve to obtain a smooth texture.

Sift To shake dry ingredients through a sieve to remove lumps.

Simmer To keep a liquid just below boiling point.

Skim To remove froth, scum or fat from the surface of stock, gravy, stews, jam etc. Use either a skimmer, a spoon or kitchen paper.

Steam To cook food in steam, usually in a steamer over rapidly boiling water.

Steep To immerse food in warm or cold liquid to soften it, and sometimes to draw out strong flavours.

Stew To cook food, such as tougher cuts of meat, in flavoured liquid which is kept at simmering point.

Stir-fry To cook small even-sized pieces of food rapidly in a little fat, tossing constantly over a high heat.

Sweat To cook chopped or sliced vegetables in a little fat without liquid in a covered pan over a low heat to soften.

Tepid The term used to describe temperature at approximately blood heat, ie 37°C (98.7°F).

Vanilla sugar Sugar in which a vanilla pod has been stored to impart its flavour.

Whipping (whisking) Beating air rapidly into a mixture either with a manual or electric whisk. Whipping usually refers to cream.

Zest The thin coloured outer layer of citrus fruit, which can be removed in fine strips with a zester.

Index